HOW TO PAINT ANYTHING

How to Paint Anything

THE COMPLETE GUIDE
TO PAINTING AND REFINISHING

HUBBARD H. COBB

Macmillan Publishing Co., Inc.
New York

Collier Macmillan Publishers
London

Copyright © 1972 by Hubbard H. Cobb

All rights reserved. No part of this book may be reproduced or transmitted in any form or by any means, electronic or mechanical, including photocopying, recording or by any information storage and retrieval system, without permission in writing from the Publisher.

Macmillan Publishing Co., Inc.
866 Third Avenue, New York, N.Y. 10022
Collier-Macmillan Canada Ltd.

Library of Congress Catalog Card Number: 75–165566

Third Printing 1974

Printed in the United States of America

698.1
C 653h

acknowledgments

I would like to thank the following organizations for providing me with general as well as product information:

Adelphi Paint & Color Works; Arsco Paint Rollers, Inc.; Behr Processing Corp.; Bull Dog Corp.; Samuel Cabot, Inc.; James B. Day & Co.; Day-Glo Color Corp.; DuPont Paint Division; Glidden; Illinois Bronze Powder & Paint Co., Inc.; International Paint Co., Inc.; The Klean Strip Co.; Kyanize Paints, Inc.; Luminall Paints, Inc.; MinWax Co.; Benjamin Moore; The Muralo Co., Inc.; Dutch Boy National Lead; National Paint, Varnish and Lacquer Association; O'Brien Corp.; Olympic Stain; Paragon Paint & Varnish Co.; PPG Industries; F. O. Pierce Co.; Permalite Plastics Corp.; Pratt & Lambert; The REZ Co.; Rust-Oleum Corp.; Rutland Products; Salmon Products; Savogran; Sapolin Paint, Inc.; Standard Dry Wall Products, Inc.; U.S. Plywood Corp.; Whitco Chemical Co.; Wm Zinsser & Co.

And my special thanks to Stanley Schuler for his invaluable assistance in the research, organization, and writing of this book.

26605

introduction

Along with many others, I have always been fascinated with paint and painting. I remember as a child watching the local house painter, Mr. Johnson, prepare his paint for a job. He would pour a quantity of white lead (it weighed a ton) into a five gallon metal container and then he would slowly add linseed oil, stirring all the time with a large wooden paddle with holes in the blade. After a spell, he would begin to add liquids and finally he'd pour in some turpentine to bring the mixture to the right brushing consistency. It would take him the better part of the morning just to mix his paint. He used just one color for both inside and outside work—white. The only exception was that window shutters were painted dark green.

If Mr. Johnson would come down from whatever special heaven good house painters go to, he'd be pretty surprised at what has happened to paints in the past couple of decades. I feel sure he would find it hard to believe that there are now paints that don't have any unpleasant odor, that can be applied over damp surfaces, that are thinned with water rather than turpentine and that dry in less than an hour, and paints with other remarkable properties. He probably wouldn't believe that paints and finishes can be applied with a roller rather than with a brush or that there are some people who do painting just with little spray cans. And he would certainly find it hard to accept the fact that today there is a paint or finish specifically designed for every surface found outside and around the house—even one for the grass on the lawn—and that there is a special paint or finish for just about every object found in the house.

But the thing that Mr. Johnson would find most difficult to accept, I am sure, is that with today's modern paints and finishes, the amateur can do as good a job of painting as most professionals.

This book, needless to say, was written for amateur painters. There are a lot of us around. Always busy, we paint houses, apartments, and boats. We paint furniture, toys, and swimming pools. We paint indoors and we paint outdoors. Some of us paint to save money, and many of us paint because we enjoy painting almost as much as saving money.

I don't want to tell you how to read or use this book, but I did write it with the idea that you would first read it through from cover to cover, absorbing general information and learning how the material has been organized. After you've done this, you can then use it as a handy encyclopedia so that when a particular surface or object needs a paint or finish, you can easily find out which paint or finish is best and how it should be applied. And please, always pay particular attention to surface preparation. As Mr. Johnson used to say, "A painter that don't take the time to get the wood right for the paint is a no damn good painter."

East Haddam, Connecticut
1971

contents

paints: general information

In this book the word "paint" is used loosely to apply to all finishes, other than wax, that are brushed, rolled, or sprayed on a surface. In actual fact, however, paint is an opaque finish that conceals the surface over which it is applied. All paint contains two essential elements—the pigment and the vehicle. The pigment provides the hiding power and color. The vehicle is the oils, or resins, in which the pigments are suspended. Paints may also contain a thinner to bring the mixture of pigments and the vehicle to the proper consistency for application and reasonably rapid drying.

Pigments are white or colored. They are made by grinding raw materials into a paste. The most familiar pigment is white lead; and it is the only pigment that can be used by itself without the addition of other pigments. It is not, however, used in its pure form around the house today because it is poisonous if eaten; but it is used in small amounts combined with other pigments.

Pigments in wide use are zinc oxide, titanium oxide, lithopone, and zinc sulphate. Red lead and zinc chromate are used extensively in primers for metal. Aluminum, bronze, and other metallic paints depend on these metals as pigments.

Through the difference in the various pigments it is possible to design paints with special characteristics. Some, for instance, are self-cleaning through a chalking process. Some will not chalk or are highly resistant to mildew or fading from exposure to the sun.

Paints are often described by the vehicle they contain rather than by the pigment. An oil paint, for example, is one in which the vehicle is linseed oil or some other type of oil. An alkyd paint is one in which the vehicle contains a high percentage of alkyd resins.

Linseed oil is one of the oldest vehicles and is still used today in many fine paints and varnishes. Other natural oils used in vehicles are tung oil, soybean oil, castor oil, and fish oil. Resins are natural as well as man made. An alkyd is a man-made resin, while the resins in shellac come from an insect.

Water is the vehicle for more and more paints made today. It has been used in the past, of course, in such paints as calcimine and whitewash, but these paints were of minor importance. Now latex—a water-base paint—threatens to sweep all others aside, and for good reasons: water is a cheap vehicle, water is odorless, and water evaporates rapidly.

Thinners are not only used to bring a paint or finish to the right consistency for application but also for cleaning equipment used for painting such as brushes, rollers, and spray guns. Among the more common thinners are turpentine, mineral spirits, and water.

TYPES OF PAINT   While there are a number of different kinds of paint and finishes used in and around the house, they can be divided roughly into five groups: (1) oil-base paints (2) alkyd paints (3) emulsion paints (of which latex is the most common) (4) water-thinned paints (5) catalytic coatings.

Oil-base paints These have been used for years for both interior and exterior work. The pigment is suspended in an oil vehicle and thinned with a solvent, such as turpentine or mineral spirits. Oil-base paints are not as popular as they once were because they are slow drying and have a strong "painty" odor, but they are still used extensively, especially in house paints for exterior work. They are also available for interior work and as enamel. They can be applied with brush, roller, or spray equipment. Turpentine or mineral spirits are used for thinning.

Alkyd paints These contain the manufactured resin known as "alkyd." They are used extensively for interior wall paints and for both interior and exterior enamel. Some types of house paint for outside walls will contain a certain percentage of alkyd resins. Alkyds are also used in some types of varnish.

Alkyd paints and finishes are easy to apply and dry more rapidly than conventional oil paints. They wash well and produce a tough coating, which is why they are so excellent for enamel.

The paints are almost odorless and should always be thinned with an odorless thinner such as mineral spirits. In spite of the lack of odor, however, they are still somewhat toxic and should be used only in well-ventilated areas. Application can be with brush, roller, or spray gun. Tools and equipment used with them can be cleaned in mineral spirits, turpentine, or benzine.

Emulsion paints These are relatively new. They comprise a family of paints made by mixing, or emulsifying, various elements, or chemicals, in water instead of dissolving them in solvents such as mineral spirits or turpentine.

Linseed-oil emulsions These are house paints made with linseed oil in a water solution that combine many of the advantages of an emulsion and a linseed-oil paint. They are easy to apply, give satisfactory adhesion to chalking surfaces, can be applied over damp surfaces, and often cover in one coat. Bare wood on which the paints are used must first be coated with a linseed-oil primer.

Latex paints These are the most popular of paints available today. Available for both exterior and interior use, latex paints are made by mixing, or emulsifying, various chemicals in water. The most common latex paints are the acrylic and vinyl, which is often called "plastic" or "PVA." Most of these are flat paints, but there are also gloss and semi-gloss enamels as well as metal primers.

Latex paints have many outstanding characteristics. First of all, they are very quick drying. In fact, they will often be dry and ready for the application of a second coat within an hour. They are almost odorless. Unlike conventional paints, they can be applied over a damp surface. Alkalis in new masonry do not damage them. Furthermore, because they are somewhat permeable to moisture, they are not likely to blister and peel if water is trapped in a wall behind them.

Another outstanding advantage of latex paints is that if certain areas are not properly coated they can be touched up very easily so that the fresh paint blends in perfectly.

Equipment used in applying latex paint—brushes, rollers,

spray guns—can be cleaned in water with or without the addition of a household detergent.

Latex paints do not adhere as well to a chalky surface as do oil paints, and for this reason the surface should be primed before application. A special latex primer should also be applied to bare wood before the latex topcoat is applied.

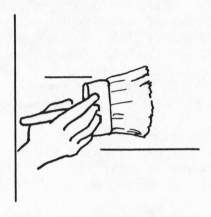

Latex paint should never be applied to bare wood. To insure good results, prime wood with a special latex primer.

Do not use latex paints if the temperature is below 45 degrees and do not store the container where the contents may freeze. In spite of the fact that latex can be applied over a damp surface it should not be applied on outside work when there is a chance of rain within the next few hours.

Although latex paints dry rapidly they are not washable until they have cured for several weeks. For this reason, when they are used in bathrooms and kitchens, take care not to get them wet for a month or so.

Water-thinned paints This term is sometimes used to describe linseed-oil emulsions and latex paints because they are thinned with water. It also applies to the non-emulsion types of paint such as calcimine and casein paints, along with whitewash, which are seldom used today. The most common water-thinned paints still in use are the Portland-cement paints, which consist of dry powders that are mixed with water before use. Portland-cement paints are used primarily for masonry surfaces.

Catalytic coatings These contain epoxy and polyurethane resins. Unlike conventional paints and finishes, catalytic coatings dry and harden through a chemical process rather than by the evaporation of solvents and thinners. They produce the toughest and most durable finish available to the home painter. They provide maximum adhesion and are highly resistant to wear, abrasion, water, acids, and solvents.

Catalytic coatings can be applied to masonry, wood, fiberglass, laminated plastics, ceramic tile, metal, porcelain, and other non-porous materials. They are excellent for marine work.

True epoxy—the most common of catalytic coatings—comes in two containers. One holds the pigment; the other, the hardener. These are mixed together just before use. Once the hardener has been added the chemical hardening process begins and the paint should be used immediately. The mixed paint cannot be stored in the container for more than a few hours. Application is with brush, roller, or spray gun.

Epoxies and other catalytic coatings are more expensive than other paints. Until they are hard—a matter of a few hours—they emit toxic and irritating fumes. They should be used only where the ventilation is good. When exposed to the weather they tend to chalk, and the colors fade somewhat, but this does not impair their function as a protective coating.

Epoxy paints cannot be applied over other types of paint, but they can be applied over an old epoxy.

Catalytic coatings are tricky to handle, so it is essential to follow the manufacturer's directions to the letter if good results are to be expected.

Paints and other finishes are further grouped according to the location and the materials for which they are designed. In selecting a paint for a particular job it is essential to use only those that the manufacturer has specified for that particular type of work.

Exterior paints These paints are designed for all general outdoor work where the finish will be exposed to the sun and weather. Included in this group are the house paints used for exterior walls, outside trim enamel for woodwork and outdoor furniture, spar varnish, and exterior pigmented stains.

Interior paints As these are designed only for inside work, they should never be used for outdoor work. In this group are wall paints and wall enamels, interior trim paints, interior varnish, and floor sealers.

Floor paints Included in this group are the special floor enamels, varnishes, and sealers that are especially formulated for use on floors and decks. They are designed to withstand abrasion and heavy wear and are the only type of finish that should be used on floors.

Masonry paints While it is often possible to use ordinary paints, such as latex, on masonry surfaces, not all paints are suitable for these materials. There are many kinds of paints and finishes exclusively designed for masonry, and these give excellent results. Other paints and finishes should be used only on masonry if the manufacturer recommends them for this purpose.

Marine paints The only kind of paint or finish to be used on boats is one designed for this purpose. Other finishes will not perform satisfactorily. Some manufacturers of house paints also have a line of marine paints, and there are also firms that specialize in this field. The wise boat-owner will always purchase the best line and grade of marine paint available.

PRIMERS   A primer is the first coat in any finishing system. Its purpose is to provide a good bond between the surface to which it is applied and subsequent coats of finish. Primers also protect the finish coats from any harmful chemical or physical reactions from the surface material.

Some types and brands of paint do not require a special primer. Often the paint used for the finish work is suitable for use as a primer if thinned according to directions.

There are three basic types of primers: (1) interior (2) exterior (3) metal.

Interior primers Interior wall primer-sealers are designed principally for plaster and gypsum board. (Gypsum board is the most accurate name for the material also known as plasterboard, sheetrock, gypsum wallboard, and wallboard.) They seal the porous surface, and this helps to insure a good bond and to prevent uneven absorption of the finish coat.

Latex emulsion primers, like latex paints, dry quickly. The equipment used with them can be washed in water. They are the best primers to use on gypsum board because they do not raise the fibers on the paper covering. They are also alkali resistant and are therefore good on masonry, new plaster, and old plaster that has become damp.

Alkyd primers and primer sealers are somewhat similar to alkyd paints in that they are odorless and dry overnight. They are not too good for new plaster unless it is completely cured or has been neutralized so that the alkalis in it are no longer active. Alkyd primers should not be used on gypsum board because they raise the fibers on the paper covering, thus requiring sanding before application of the finish paint.

Alkali-resistant primers are usually based on chlorinated rubber or some similar material. They are primarily designed for surfaces that contain alkali, such as damp or partly cured plaster or masonry.

Fast-drying primer-sealers have a shellac base with a white pigment added. (They are also called stain killers.) They dry within one hour and are excellent for walls, ceilings, and interior woodwork. Unlike other primers, you can apply them in subfreezing weather.

Enamel undercoaters are special primers used with enamel. They provide a hard, tight, smooth film and are usually white but may be tinted to any color. See enamel undercoaters.

Softwood-plywood primer-sealers are phenolic resin penetrating sealers used to keep the grain of plywood from showing through the finish paint. See phenolic resin primer-sealers.

Clear wood-sealers are designed to seal the pores of wood without impairing the natural appearance. They can be used as a complete finishing system or as a primer for a clear finish such as varnish.

Clear masonry-sealers are similar to the above but used on masonry.

Exterior primers These should be used on all new wood and over old paint that is in poor condition. They include the following:

Alkyd primers are used under oil-base house paints and latex paints. You can apply them to new wood as well as to paint that is heavily chalked.

Latex primers differ somewhat from conventional latex paints in that they take longer to dry—usually overnight. They are, however, water thinned and therefore have the advantages that go with a so-called water paint.

Metal primers These are required to insure a good bond between the finish paint and the metal; and in the case of iron and steel, they also prevent formation of rust. While it is not always essential to prime interior metal that is not exposed to moisture, the chances of a successful paint job will be improved if a primer is used.

Red lead is the oldest and most familiar metal primer. It is available in an oil as well as an alkyd base. Red lead is especially good if the surface has not been given perfect preparation and some rust remains. It is slow to dry and does not stand up alone for very long; consequently it should be topcoated as soon as it is dry.

Zinc chromate is available in oil and alkyd bases, too. The primers dry faster and harder than red lead and are the best for use on aluminum.

Zinc dust primers are recommended for galvanized steel.

Latex-inhibitive primers are water thinned and easy to apply. They must have a topcoat, which will keep out all moisture.

Portland-cement paints containing oil are also used to prime galvanized steel.

PAINT THINNERS   As a rule, modern paints and other finishes should be applied as they come from the can. Thinning is done only if the finish is too thick to apply easily (note that dripless paints are deliberately made very thick and should be used that way) or if application of unusually thin coats is required to give the desired effect (as in French polishing). Follow the directions on the can about how much thinner to use. The best thinners to use are as follows:

In solvent-based paints, enamels, and varnishes: turpentine or odorless thinner (mineral spirits).

In water-based paints: water.

In shellac and other alcohol-based materials: denatured alcohol.

In lacquer: lacquer thinner.

The same thinners are used for cleaning up spills and cleaning brushes, rollers, and spray guns.

Mineral spirits Sometimes called petroleum spirits or petroleum distillates, this is an inexpensive and usually odorless liquid used for thinning solvent-base paints, cleaning brushes, and cleaning surfaces to be painted. It has generally replaced turpentine in home painting.

Turpentine Turpentine is used to thin oil-base paints and finishes, to clean the utensils used for applying these finishes, and to clean surfaces before painting. Because of its strong odor it should not be used for thinning odorless paints.

Gum spirits of turpentine is the best and most expensive type of "turps" and is recommended for thinning paints. Steamed distilled wood-turpentine should be used for the less critical cleaning jobs. They are, however, interchangeable.

Benzine A petroleum derivative very similar to naphtha, which can be used to clear surfaces that are to be painted or given a clear finish. It is particularly good for removing wax and furniture polish and for cleaning wood, since it does not raise the grain, as water does. It can also be used for cleaning paint brushes.

Because benzine is flammable, it should not be used near a flame or by anyone who is smoking. And don't scrub it on with steel wool.

Alcohol Alcohol is the carrier, or liquid, in shellac and several pigmented paints and sealers. It is also the base of alcohol wood-stains.

In painting, denatured alcohol is generally used to thin the above finishes, but in a pinch you can use rubbing alcohol. Brushes and other equipment used to apply an alcohol-base finish should be soaked briefly in alcohol and then washed with mild soap and water.

Kerosene This is a low-cost solvent. It should not be used as a thinner in place of mineral spirits or turpentine unless the paint manufacturer so specifies. As kerosene does not evaporate quickly or leave a gummy deposit, it makes a good liquid in which to suspend paint brushes for cleaning and storage.

GENERAL INFORMATION   Because of the great advances in paint technology, there is a wide difference in the composition, types, and brands of paint. Many are incompatible, and when they are applied over one another, problems arise.

Paint systems The best way to insure good results is to follow what paint manufacturers call a painting "system." All this means is that the undercoater, primer, and finish paint you use for a given job should work together. Most paint-makers specify on the label the correct primer to use with that particular paint or the correct paint to use with that particular primer. The safest approach is to use not only the type of paint recommended by the manufacturer but his brand as well.

Toxicity The toxic, or poisonous, effect that paint has when inhaled varies from one type and brand of finish to another. Some are harmless; others are quite dangerous. Unfortunately you can't tell which is which. Many odorless paints are just as lethal as those with a strong smell.

It follows that when you apply a finish of any kind, you must work in a well-ventilated room.

Wear a mask or respirator when using a spray gun. However this isn't necessary with an aerosol paint.

And don't swallow the stuff, obviously.

Hiding power The hiding power of paints varies with the amount and type of pigment they contain. For instance, one-coat house paints have more hiding power than conventional house paints because they contain more pigment; dark-colored paints have more hiding power than light-colored paints because of the opacity of the pigment.

Hiding power is an important point to consider when you buy paints because it can mean a saving in the cost of the paint as well as in application time and labor. Why put on two coats if one does as well? Furthermore, those with extra pigment usually last longer.

Selection and buying The type of finish you should buy depends on what you are finishing, what the conditions are that it will be exposed to, and what effect you wish to achieve. See the entries for the materials and objects you are working on.

The amount of paint you should order depends on how much coverage the paint gives, on how large an area is to be covered, on what the surface is, and on how many coats must be applied.

The coverage of the many paints and other finishes sold today varies greatly. For example, one gallon of an epoxy primer made by one manufacturer for use on concrete and cinder blocks will cover only about 75 square feet, whereas a gallon of the epoxy enamel applied over the primer will cover about 225 square feet. Similarly, one gallon of an acrylic latex pigmented exterior-stain will cover only about 200 square feet, whereas a gallon of acrylic latex house-paint will cover about 450.

The labels on many paint cans contain information about the coverage you can expect. Ask the paint dealer about the others. Then, if you know the size of the area you are going to paint, it will be an easy matter for you and the dealer to figure out approximately how much paint you will need.

Actually, underordering is usually smarter than overordering, for as long as you are buying a ready-mixed paint or one that the dealer mixes to the paint manufacturer's formula, you can always go back to the store and order more. But if you have paint mixed to a special color it is better to overorder slightly, because if you should run out the paint dealer might not be able to match the paint exactly.

Estimating paint requirements The amount of paint or finish required is based on three factors: the area in square feet that is to be covered, the condition of the surface (smooth, rough, or porous), and the number of coats required. If you have this information you can usually determine yourself from reading the label on the container how much paint to order or, if you give the information to your paint dealer, he can do it for you.

ESTIMATING SQUARE FEET To do this, measure the length and the width or height in feet and multiply these two figures together. The sum will be the total area in square feet. For walls, multiply the length by the height. For floors, multiply the length by the width. To estimate the requirements for windows and doors, measure the height and width to get the total number of square feet and then count the number of units involved and multiply these two figures together.

To figure the area of the outside of a house, measure the perimeter and the height from the foundation to the roof line. Multiply the two figures together. If the house has a gable end, either add two feet to the overall height of the house or measure the gable from the eave line to the peak and multiply these together and add to the total.

Make a note of the condition of the surface or the type of surface you are going to paint. Masonry is very porous so it will take considerably more paint than wood. Narrow wood-siding will

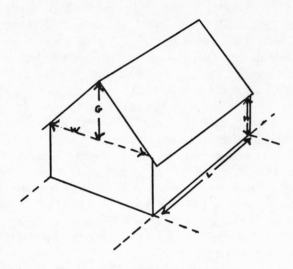

To estimate the amount of paint required for the outside of a house, first determine in feet the length (L), height (H), width (W), and the height of the gable end (G).

require more paint than wide siding. Shingles require more paint than smooth siding.

If you are changing color, you will probably require two coats, but if you are using the same color and the old paint is in good condition, one will usually be adequate.

Give all this information to your paint dealer so he can intelligently advise you on how much paint will be needed.

Mixing If you need a special paint color let a paint dealer mix it for you. He has the equipment and, presumably, the know-how to do the job just right and in short order. And if he fails to achieve the desired result, the unusable can of paint is his loss, not yours.

However, if you insist on trying your hand, here is how to go about it:

First you must figure out exactly how much paint you will require and order the full amount; otherwise, if you try mixing the paint in small batches, you will almost certainly discover that one batch doesn't match another.

The base paint you order may be white or it may be fairly close to the color you are aiming for. For example, if you want orange it's easier to start with a clear yellow than with white.

The tinting colors are high-strength colorants sold in tubes or squeeze bottles. For oil paints you can use colors-in-oil, which are available in tubes. Special colorants are used for water-base paints. But so-called universal tinting colors, which are compatible with all kinds of paint, are now available.

Do not add the tinting colors directly to the base paint because they may not mix in thoroughly. You should instead pour a little base paint into a jar and mix the tinting colors into that. Then add the mixture to the full can. Continue in this way until the desired color has been attained.

If you need a large quantity of paint, all the cans of base paint should first be mixed together in a 2- to 5-gallon container.

Storage No one has yet found a sure way to store paint so that a skin does not form on the surface. The most reliable procedure is to pry off the can lid very carefully so you do not bend it or damage the edges. Then, when you have finished painting, clean all the paint off the top edges of the can with a paper towel; press the lid squarely into place with your hands; center your foot on it, and press down hard two or three times with your foot pointed in different directions. Try to maintain even pressure on all edges of the lid.

If the lid on a can is damaged in any way or the top of the can is not free of paint, you may be able to compensate for the fact that the lid will not close tight by placing the can in a plastic kitchen bag, squeezing out all of the air, and knotting the top.

All paints should be stored in a well-ventilated room at moderate temperature. Keep them well away from the furnace, water heater, or other fire hazards.

How long any stored paint or other finish will remain usable depends on the finish itself and the storage conditions. Two-part epoxy paints, for instance, become unusable about eight hours after they are mixed, though it is possible to extend this time a bit by putting them in a refrigerator. Shellac may not last longer than six months. By contrast, clear lacquer lasts a long time.

Generally, if the finish contains a pigment, the pigment settles to the bottom of the can, forms a sludge, and then finally sets into a stiff putty that will neither break up nor dissolve.

When using a paint that has been stored for a year or more the difficulty of stirring it to a smooth, workable liquid will give you a pretty good lead as to whether it is still usable. But the best way to check the situation is to brush a little of the paint on a test surface and see how long it takes to dry to the desired film. If the drying time is unusually long, throw the paint away.

LABELING PAINTS This is an important phase of storing paints that is too often overlooked. It should be obvious, however, that if a can of paint is worth saving in the first place, you should know where it has been used. This is very easy to forget, especially if you have several cans of paint that are close in color.

It follows that before you store a can of paint you should note on it what it is, if that is not self-evident (for example: pale-blue alkyd semi-gloss). Also note where it has been used and the month and year it was purchased. Use a china-marking pencil or a felt pen.

You should also dab a spot of the paint on the can.

POT LIFE The pot life of paint is the period of its usability. Paint dealers sometimes refer to the shelf life of paint, which means the same thing.

Preparing paint for use If you buy a new can of paint that you intend to use within a few days, have the dealer shake it up on his shaking machine.

Whether a pigmented finish has been shaken or not, you should stir it well just before using it. The inch-wide wooden paint paddles that paint dealers give away are as good as anything for this purpose, but any clean, splinter-free stick will do. If the paint can is full almost to the rim, pour some of the paint into a paint pail and stir each batch separately until well homogenized. Then pour one batch into the other—back and forth—stirring between pourings until the entire lot of paint is blended and smooth.

On large jobs professional painters sometimes pour all gallon cans of the same color and type together in a five-gallon pail for stirring. You can do this, too, but unless there are several people helping with your painting, it is not likely that you will use more than a gallon in a day. Therefore you don't gain anything by this practice.

If a skin has formed on paint, it must be removed before the paint is stirred. Sometimes, if you are careful, you can cut the skin away from the sides of the can and lift it out in one piece. If you do this, hold the skin over the can and let as much of the vehicle and pigment drip from it as possible. Generally, however, the skin will shred or break so that you can't get it all out. In this case, after the paint has been stirred strain it through cheesecloth or a kitchen wire-mesh strainer into another clean can or pail.

Paint must also be strained (even though it may not have a skin) if it contains lumps and specks. This is particularly important for paint that is to be sprayed. Use several thicknesses of cheesecloth. These can be tied over the tip of the can or spread out in a kitchen strainer set in the can. A nylon-mesh stocking fitted over the top of the can is also good. Pour the paint through slowly and don't try to hurry the process by stirring because that may force some of the unwanted particles through the cloth.

Once paint has been strained don't pour it back into the old can until that has been thoroughly cleaned.

Some paints need to be stirred occasionally while you are using them. All should be stirred at the start of each painting operation.

If you are not using paint directly out of the can (as, for example, when you apply it with a roller) keep the lid on the can to exclude dust and prevent drying of the paint.

CLEAR FINISHES These generally do not need stirring. In fact, varnish should not be stirred because that creates bubbles that may show up in the surface film. Varnish and penetrating floor-sealers sometimes need straining, however, because they have formed a skin.

Cleaning up after painting Four steps are called for:

1. Clean the area in which you have been painting. Drips and splatters are easier to remove when paint is wet than when it is dry. Use a soft, absorbent rag or paper towels. You may also need a rag dipped in the thinner used for the paint.

Don't assume that because you have covered floors and furniture with drop cloths that paint may not have gotten underneath. And don't forget to look for paint that you may have tracked into adjoining rooms on the soles of your shoes.

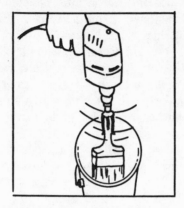

Special attachments can be used on an electric drill for cleaning brushes. There are also attachments that can be used to mix paint.

2. Clean the rim of the paint can before putting on the lid.
3. Clean your brushes, roller, and spray gun.
4. Clean your hands and face. The jellied hand-cleaners sold by paint stores are the kindest to the skin and in most cases amazingly effective. If they don't do a perfect job, use the appropriate thinner.

Paint as a vapor barrier   Any paint or clear finish such as an alkyd, latex, varnish, or shellac will bar the passage of moisture vapor from inside the house to the cold outdoors. It is necessary only that the paint or clear finish be applied in a continuous film to all inside surfaces of all exterior walls: for example, ceilings under the roof and floors over unheated crawl spaces. Apply two coats to insure complete, unbroken coverage.

If the paint on the exterior of an old house is blistering because water has soaked into the wall behind it, application of a paint or clear-finish vapor barrier is often an easy way to correct the problem.

Special finishes   The following finishes are described under separate entries: antique, crackle, driftwood, heather mahogany, honey maple, limed oak, marble, pickled pine, silver oak, spatter.

enamel, clear finishes,
and stains

ENAMEL   This is a special kind of pigmented finish designed to produce a very smooth, hard coating that is easily cleaned and highly resistant to weather and to wear.

Enamels are available for both interior and exterior use. A large number are designed for special purposes such as wood and masonry floors, outdoor furniture, metal, farm and garden equipment, automobiles, radiators, kitchen appliances, and so forth. While many can be used for several purposes, it is always best to use enamels that are designed for the particular surface involved.

Enamels are available in gloss, semigloss, and eggshell, or flat, finishes. The two types in common use are the alkyd solvent-thinned enamel and the newer latex enamel. Both give good results.

Enamels can be applied with a brush, spray gun, mohair roller, or mohair applicator pad. You will not, however, get a very smooth finish when a gloss enamel is applied with a roller or applicator. Enamel is also available in aerosol containers and these are excellent for small jobs.

For most jobs a brush is the usual method of application. Use a high quality enamel-brush—one with a chisel rather than blunt tip. The main difference between applying enamel and ordinary paint is that you will fill your brush a bit more with enamel, flow it on the surface, and brush it out less. Enamels often dry rather rapidly, so any runs or sags should be picked up immediately before the paint has a chance to set.

Enamel undercoaters   These are applied to a surface before it is coated with enamel. They produce a low-gloss, tight film that prevents the penetration of the final finish. While they may be used under any pigmented finish, they are particularly important to the attainment of a very smooth finish in gloss and semi-gloss enamels.

Undercoaters are nearly always white but may be tinted for use under colored topcoats. They may be used as a primer on metals where exposure is relatively mild and no rusting is expected. Latex, alkyd, and varnish undercoaters are also available.

While flat paints are often used in place of enamel undercoaters, they do not perform so well. This is especially true when a very smooth-gloss finish is desired.

After the undercoater is dry it should be sanded lightly, and light sanding is required between coats of enamel.

CLEAR FINISHES   Unlike paints, these are free of pigments and therefore do not hide the surface to which they are applied. But because they don't contain pigments, they do not stand up as long as paints do when they are exposed to sun and weather. They are, however, used for a variety of finishing jobs, both inside and outside.

Among the clear finishes are varnish, shellac, lacquer, penetrating floor and wood sealers, urethane coatings, and clear epoxy coatings. They are also called natural finishes.

Varnish   This is a clear, solvent-thinned finish used on floors, furniture, interior and exterior wood trim, boats, wood paneling, and other wood surfaces.

There are many types of varnish. Some are clearer than others. Some are more resistant to moisture and wear. Some have a high gloss, while others have a semigloss or flat finish. An all-purpose varnish does not exist.

For exterior and marine work only top-grade spar varnish should be used. Floors require a special floor varnish. Furniture and trim are usually finished with an interior or semigloss varnish. Where alcohol may be present, bar varnish should be used.

Varnish is best applied with a good bristle brush, ideally one that is used only for varnish; no matter how well it is cleaned, any paint left in the bristles may discolor the varnish. Varnish may also be applied with a pad of lint-free cloth.

Do not stir varnish before use; this creates bubbles. When using a brush dip it into the varnish only a third of its length, always flowing the varnish on liberally with a minimum number of brush strokes. To remove excess varnish from the brush don't drag the bristles across the rim of the can. This causes tiny bubbles to form and will make it almost impossible to achieve a smooth finish. Instead, tap the tips of the bristles against the inside of the can.

When brushing varnish apply only a moderate amount of pressure. Do not bend the bristles. Flow on with the grain, then brush across the grain. Finish by stroking lightly with the bristle tips, using an almost dry brush and working with the grain. This helps to assure a coating of uniform depth and appearance and with few brush marks.

To apply varnish with a cloth pad, dip the pad into the varnish, getting a generous quantity into the cloth. Spread the varnish with long strokes, parallel to the grain. Do not rub hard and make no attempt to work the varnish into the surface. Wipe up runs and sags at once, since varnish seldom levels itself out.

When more than one finish coat is applied sand lightly before putting on the next.

As varnish is a moderately slow-drying finish it should never be applied in a dusty location outside, especially when there is a breeze. You should also avoid working in a very dusty room. It is a sound idea to vacuum thoroughly a day before applying varnish.

Spar varnish Also called exterior or outside varnish, this is designed mainly for exterior and marine use. It is the most weather-resistant varnish available and is the only type (other than urethane varnish) that should be used on exterior work. It is not suitable for floors and furniture, however.

Shellac Shellac is a clear finish made by reducing natural resins in alcohol. It dries dust-free in about 15 minutes and is ready for a second coat or sanding in about two hours. It forms an excellent base for many other finishes, prevents knots and sappy streaks in wood from bleeding, and seals fresh plaster patches and gypsum board that is to be papered. It is often used as a final finish on fine furniture, provided it is protected with wax. And it is recommended by shellac manufacturers as a wood-floor finish.

There are two types of shellac: orange and white. The former is less expensive and because of its color should be used only under opaque finishes. White shellac is one of the most nearly colorless, clear finishes available. (Shellac containing white or black pigment is also on the market and is used as a sealer or final finish.)

When buying shellac look for a date on the can. This tells when the shellac was produced. If it is over six months old it may not dry properly, if at all. Before accepting it you should ask the dealer to test it on a scrap of wood. Shellac that has been sitting on a shelf in your own home for a long time should also be given a drying test before you use it.

Shellac can be applied by brush or with a spray can. For most purposes a 3-pound cut is recommended, and it is commonly sold in this concentration. But you can also buy a 4-pound cut. To reduce a 4-pound to a 3-pound cut, add ½ pint denatured alcohol to 1 quart shellac. A 1-pound cut is achieved by adding 2 quarts alcohol to 1 quart 4-pound cut shellac or 3 pints alcohol to 1 quart 3-pound cut shellac.

Brushes and equipment used with shellac are best cleaned with denatured alcohol and then washed in soap and water.

Shellac should be applied with a full brush. Just before it has set but while it is still wet, go back over it lightly with the tip of the brush to remove bubbles. If any areas are missed don't try to touch them up while the shellac is wet; wait until it is fully dry and then recoat.

When applying several coats of shellac go over each coat when dry with fine sandpaper or steel wool. It is better to build up a shellac finish in several thin coats than one or two thick coats.

Keep a shellac finish clean with a rag dampened in a little water or detergent solution. If the finish is stained or water spotted, clean it with denatured alcohol. Rubbing with alcohol also helps to conceal scratches, because the alcohol softens the shellac and allows it to flow together again. If a shellacked surface is badly damaged, remove it entirely with sandpaper and then apply several very thin coats.

Lacquer Lacquer is a very fast-drying finish that contains nitrocellulose. Used primarily on furniture, it produces a hard, tough, glossy finish. It is thinned with lacquer thinner, which is also used for cleaning your application equipment. Both clear, or water-white, and pigmented lacquers are sold.

Lacquer should not be applied over most other paints or finishes because it may act as a paint remover. It can, however, be applied over shellac; and it can serve as a base for all paints and finishes.

The best application method is with a spray gun or spray can. But slower drying lacquers known as brushing lacquers are applied with a brush. The brush should be well filled with lacquer, which is then flowed on the surface with rapid strokes. Do not brush lacquer out very much.

Lacquer is highly inflammable and should not be used around an open flame.

Sealers Sealers are oil-base materials—usually clear, but sometimes colored—designed to penetrate the surfaces to which they are applied and thus seal the pores, prevent absorption of water and stains, and simplify cleaning. They may be used alone or under other finishes to prevent these from entering the wood. In this way, they make for a smoother, more even final finish.

The sealers in most common use are penetrating floor-sealers. But there are also sealers for use on siding and exterior woodwork that is to be left natural, on furniture, on plywood (to control the wild grain), and on masonry.

Sealers are usually applied with a brush so you can work them into the wood. As a rule, two coats are used if no other finish is applied.

Phenolic resin primer-sealers Formulated primarily for plywood made of Douglas fir and other softwoods, these sealers are designed to penetrate the pores of the wood and equalize the density of the grain. Brush them on wood that is to be stained or painted. They are available clear or with a white or colored pigment.

Fillers Before the finish is applied, these are often used for filling the pores of open-grained woods, such as oak, walnut, and mahogany. Most fillers come in paste form and are clear or colored, depending on the requirements. They are applied after the wood has been stained. Thin about 50 per cent with turpentine;

brush on with and then across the grain. Allow the filler to stand for several minutes or until the surface turns dull; then rub off across the grain and with the grain. Smooth with medium sandpaper or steel-wool the wood after the filler is dry.

When a filler is desired for close-grained woods, apply a couple of coats of thinned white shellac.

Water repellents These are used to seal the pores of masonry and wood so that moisture will not be readily absorbed. They are liquids and can be applied with a brush or spray gun. Two types of water repellents are available.

One that contains silicone resins in a solvent is used to keep water out of masonry walls. Because it is transparent and colorless, it does not change the natural color of the walls. These qualities make it most suitable for a brick wall.

Silicone water-repellents are not actually waterproofers (although manufacturers may imply that they are) because they cannot stop water from getting into the walls through cracks. But they are excellent damp-proofers, meaning that they stop moisture from seeping through the tiny pores found in all masonry.

If you use a silicone repellent, you must make repeat applications every five years to insure continual effectiveness.

The second type of water repellent is pentachlorophenol woodpreservative. It is highly recommended as a natural finish on wood, especially redwood because it modifies the weathering process this wood goes through when used outdoors. Usually only one initial application of two coats is needed. In very humid climates, however, you should apply another coat whenever the redwood begins to darken. *See* redwood.

Bleaches Bleaching is a process used to lighten the natural color of wood, to lighten wood that has been previously stained, or to remove discolorations that have penetrated so deeply that they defy sanding.

Bleaching is frequently required in refinishing furniture. If dark woods are to be given a blond finish, for example, they must first be lightened. Bleaching is also often required in floor finishing to remove stains.

The bleaching agent must be applied to bare wood, as a surface coating will keep the bleach from the wood. Care should be taken to keep bleach off any surface that is not to be bleached. Since all bleaching agents are strong, wear rubber gloves when working with them.

Several applications of a bleaching agent may be needed to produce the desired results. Light-colored woods will naturally respond more readily than the dark ones.

Because a bleach raises the grain, the wood must be sanded well after bleaching.

OXALIC ACID   This is an inexpensive bleach that is good for all but the most difficult operations. Oxalic-acid crystals are available at drugstores, as well as many paint and hardware stores. A good solution is made by dissolving ½ cup of the crystals in 1 quart of hot water. Use a glass or plastic container. Apply the solution liberally (while hot) with a brush or sponge. Allow it to dry, and then brush off the crystals. Repeat the process until you have achieved the color you want. When finished, neutralize the surface by wiping with a solution of 1 part household ammonia in 10 parts water or with 1 cup of borax in 1 quart of water or with denatured alcohol. Then wash with clear water and allow to dry for at least 24 hours before applying the finish.

Avoid inhaling the dust from the surface when sanding prior to finishing.

BLEACHING OILS   These are commercial bleaches with a little gray pigment added. They are used on exterior siding, wood decks, fences, and so forth to hasten the natural weathering process.

COMMERCIAL WOOD BLEACHES   These are the strongest and most expensive bleaching agents. They come in two containers. Apply them according to the manufacturer's directions.

LIQUID LAUNDRY BLEACH   Bleaches, such as Clorox, can be very effective in bleaching out stains previously applied to wood, as well as other discolorations that are not too intense. Use the bleach just as it comes from the bottle. When the desired result has been obtained rinse with fresh water and allow to dry.

STAINS
Stains are used on wood to bring out the natural color and grain or to darken or change the color without concealing the grain and texture.

Since stains are absorbed into the wood, they must be applied to bare wood. Many stains must be protected by a coat of shellac, varnish, or lacquer.

Stains come in a wide range of colors and tones. It is always best first to test a stain on a scrap of wood similar to that which you are working on or on an inconspicuous section of the work itself. After it dries apply the finish coating. Only in this way can you determine what the exact final effect will be.

If the test area is blotchy or uneven because of the characteristics of the wood grain, apply a coat of very thin white shellac before the stain.

It is always safer to use a stain that is on the light side rather than on the dark side. If the first application turns out too light, another coat can be applied. If the stain is too dark, however, it can be lightened only by bleaching or sanding.

Stains must be applied to wood that has been sanded smooth and clean. They can be applied with a brush or with a pad of lint-free cloth. Apply the stain to a rather small area and allow it to stand for a few minutes; then wipe it with a cloth to get a uniform color. The end grain of wood will absorb more stain than other surfaces, so use stain sparingly; or wet the end grain with mineral spirits just before staining.

Most stains must dry overnight—preferably for 24 hours—before the surface is ready for a finish.

Oil stains Clear oil-stains have been used for many, many years to stain furniture, wood paneling, and woodwork that is to be given a clear finish. But in recent years stains have shot up in popularity for exterior wood finishing.

Two basic types of oil stain are available: clear and opaque. Clear stain changes the color of wood but does not conceal the grain, texture, and imperfections in it. The opaque, or pigmented, stain, on the other hand, not only changes the color of wood but also partially obscures the wood. In this respect it is somewhat like a paint, but there are several important differences. For one thing, stain penetrates the wood to a certain extent, whereas paint merely lies on top. As noted, the stain does not completely hide the wood grain or surface texture. Finally, because of its penetrating ability, a gallon of stain does not give so much coverage as a gallon of paint, but you don't have to renew the finish as often (this is particularly true if the wood is rough-sawn).

Opaque stains are best applied with a brush, although you can use a roller or spray gun. Just make sure the surface is clean and dry; then brush the stain on with the grain and let it dry for a couple of days. Two coats are necessary on raw wood, but one is usually enough over old stain.

Two questions that are often asked about pigmented stains are: Can they be applied over a painted surface and can you make a stain by diluting paint with a thinner? The answer to the first is "yes," provided that the old paint has weathered away almost to nothing. The answer to the second is "no." No thinner used to dilute paint has the excellent penetrating characteristics of the special oils used in prepared stains.

Clear oil-stains used outdoors on house walls and on your finest furniture indoors are applied in the same way. A brush is usually employed, but if you don't want to stain the wood too deeply use a rag. This puts on less stain than a brush and produces a more even effect.

Let the stain soak into the wood for a few minutes; then wipe it off with a clean cloth. Try to rub out lap marks. If the color is not as deep as you want, make a second application in the same way. Let the stain dry for 48 hours at least before you over-coat it with varnish, shellac, or lacquer.

Alcohol stains Alcohol stains are the most difficult clear stains to use because they penetrate and dry in a twinkling. Brush them on small sections and rub them off almost immediately with a clean rag. The final finish can be applied over them within a couple of hours.

Alcohol stains are most often used under lacquer.

Water stains Water stains are more difficult to work with than oil stains, and it is advisable for the amateur to bypass them.

To make a stain, dissolve an analine dye in warm water. Moisten the surface and then apply with a brush, using long straight strokes. You must work quite fast because the stain penetrates and dries rapidly. Slow or uneven application will result in brush lap marks. As soon as one area has been completed, wipe off the excess stain with a clean cloth.

Let the wood dry for 12 hours or more; then sand it with fine sandpaper to take down the grain, which the water raises.

Non-grain-raising stains These are similar to water stains except that instead of dissolving dye powders in hot water you use a special solvent made by the dye manufacturer. Since the solvent does not raise the grain of the wood, sanding after staining is unnecessary.

Varnish stain This is a combination of stain and varnish. Its great advantage is that it completes two operations in one. But it does not produce a very attractive or durable finish and is used only when economy or speed of application is a prime consideration. You will often run into it, for instance, in summer cottages and on rough furniture.

The material is available in several colors. Apply it with a brush or spray gun.

Dipping Dipping is a good way to apply a clear stain to a fairly small article that can be completely immersed in one or two steps. You can also apply paint, but unless you then go over the article with a brush to remove the excess, the paint will form an undesirably heavy film, and a blob of it will hang from the bottom of the article.

specialized paints and finishes

There is a wide variety of specialized paints, finishes, and allied paint products available today. Many of them are designed for a very specific purpose, and some can be used for a variety of work.

It is a good idea to be aware of the existence of these specialized products. Many hardware stores and even some paint shops will not have them in stock and therefore won't suggest their use. They might suggest some other product that is not as well suited for the job as one designed for that purpose alone. But if you know what you want, you can either have them order it for you or shop around until you find a store that does carry exactly what you require.

Aerosol paints A wide assortment of paints and finishes is available in aerosol spray cans. They include:

Acrylic	Polyurethane
Antique finish	Rust inhibitor
Chalkboard paint	Sealer
Enamel	Semi-gloss
Epoxy	Shellac
Fabric paint	Stain
Flat	Undercoater
Fluorescent	Varnish
Frosting for glass	Varnish stain
Gloss	Wax
Hammered finish	Wrinkle finish
Lacquer	Wrought-iron finish
Metal primer	

While aerosols are expensive to use on large surfaces, they are ideal for small jobs and touch-up work and for surfaces that cannot easily be coated with brush or roller. Spray painting also avoids lap marks and brush streaking. An obvious advantage is that of minimum clean-up.

Most aerosol paints need to be shaken well before using. Unless this is done the paint may come out too thin or the pressure may be used up before the paint. Shake the container for at least 30 seconds and then hold it by the top and swirl it around until the metal ball inside is at the bottom. This helps to insure blending of the pigments, which often settle at the bottom.

A surface to be coated with an aerosol-spray finish must be clean and smooth, just as for brush or roller application. It is best to place the piece in a horizontal position to avoid running and insure even distribution of paint. (Note, however, that some aerosols will operate properly only if held more or less in an upright position.) Spray in a well-ventilated area. Don't spray outdoors on windy days.

The spray nozzle should be held 8 to 12 inches from the work surface. Keep the nozzle parallel to the work. If you swing it in an arc the coating will be uneven. Best results are achieved by spraying very thin coats and allowing ample drying time between them.

When finished with a job, clean the nozzle by inverting the can and pressing down on the cap a few times for just a second. This will send the propellant through to remove any traces of paint.

Aluminum paint   A paint made with fine flakes of aluminum suspended in either a varnish or asphalt base. The varnish type of paint is used extensively as a primer sealer to prevent stains from bleeding through the topcoat of paint. It can also be used for finishing purposes.

Asphalt-base aluminum paint is used as a roof coating.

Barn paints   Barn paints are similar to oil-base house paints but are more likely to contain vehicle modifications, such as resin. They usually employ red iron-oxide as the chief hiding pigment. They are, however, available in other colors, such as green and black. They are designed to give a uniform appearance over poorly prepared and non-uniform surfaces, but do not stand up as well as conventional house paints.

Blister-resistant paints   These are oil- or water-thinned paints designed to resist blistering and peeling caused by moisture getting into the wood behind the paint film. To be effective the paints must be applied to bare wood, according to the manufacturer's directions. They will not be effective if applied over old paint that is blistering and peeling.

Block fillers These are a relatively thick composition that is used to fill the voids in masonry blocks that are to be painted. It reduces the number of finish coats required. The most common block filler is a latex, which can be applied with brush or roller and may be used on a damp surface.

Calcimine Calcimine, or kalsomine, is an inexpensive water-thinned interior paint that was popular some years ago for ceilings and occasionally for walls. It is seldom used today but may still be found in older dwellings. Old calcimine must be removed before any new paint is applied. Even a fresh coat of calcimine cannot be applied over an old coat.

It is a simple matter to test a surface to determine if the finish is calcimine: just rub it with a cloth or sponge wet in warm water. If the finish comes off, it is calcimine and the entire surface should be washed to remove all traces of it.

Casein paints This is a type of water paint once widely used for interior walls and ceilings but now replaced by the more efficient latex paints. However, casein paints are often recommended today for painting acoustical ceilings because they do not fill the voids in the tiles to the same degree as other paints.

Cement-based paints See Portland-cement paints. There are also very thick cement-base materials that are used to fill and seal the voids in masonry; but these are more properly called coatings than paints. They are excellent waterproofing compounds used in basements, exterior walls, swimming pools, cisterns, and the like. They are now sold in a variety of pastel colors.

Chalkboard paint Available in aerosol cans, this finish can be used to refinish factory-made boards or to convert any smooth surface into a chalkboard. Simply make certain that the surface to be painted is clean and dry. Then apply the paint in light, even coats.

Chlorinated rubber paints See solvent-thinned rubber-base paints.

Colors-in-oil Used for tinting and changing the color of

ready-mixed paints, colors-in-oil come in tubes and have the consistency of a thick paste. Only a small amount is needed to produce a marked change in color.

Colors-in-oil can be mixed into all paints except those with a water base. Special color concentrates must be used with the latter. *See* paint, mixing.

Dope Dope is a special lacquer product smelling like banana oil, which is used primarily on model airplanes, cars, etc. It must be applied with a brush only to bare surfaces; applied over any other finish, it will eat right through. Dope, however, is frequently used as a primer over which ordinary lacquer, enamel, and other finishes can be safely applied.

For priming most materials use a clear dope that is easy to sand (a sanding sealer). On balsa wood and other porous materials, use another clear dope containing a filler. Finish coats are applied with pigmented dope.

When using dope, thin it only with the special thinner designated by the manufacturer. Never mix the dope or thinner with any other finish.

Driers A drier is a clear liquid that may be added to solvent-base finishes to shorten the drying time. Only very small amounts are needed. For varnish and enamel, for example, you use less than 4 ounces per gallon; for paints, less than 8 ounces. The exact amounts are indicated on the container label.

Dripless paints These paints have a very thick, somewhat jelly-like consistency and should not be thinned. Despite their appearance they brush out easily. But it is an exaggeration to say they are dripless, because if you overload your brush or brush them out carelessly, they will splatter slightly and drop big globs.

In other words, don't neglect to put down drop cloths.

Farm equipment enamels Basically similar to exterior trim enamels, but because their use is largely on metal, they often contain a hard-drying resin, along with rust-inhibiting pigment. They are similar in composition to automotive enamels.

Fireproof paints Fireproof paints are rare and have little or no place in the home. However, one that has been used in the space program shows considerable promise as a coating on the inner metal surfaces of furnace fireboxes. Fireboxes protected with the paint are highly resistant to the deteriorating effects of high heat and acids given off by burning fuel.

Fire-retardant paints   These are known as intumescent coatings. This means that when the paint is exposed to heat, it swells and foams up to form an insulating barrier between the heat source and the material to which the paint is applied. Thus the paint delays ignition of the painted material but does not prevent it.

Fire-retardant paints are not widely used in homes but are useful for protecting certain areas. You might, for example, use them on a wood ceiling over a furnace or in rooms occupied by invalids, elderly people, and infants.

Most of the paints have a flat or low-luster finish but are reasonably washable. They are generally not so attractive in appearance as conventional paints, however.

Flat paints   Paints with a matte, or dull, finish, these are preferred for most walls and ceilings because they are more restful to look at than gloss paints. But they are the least washable of all paints.

Fluorescent paints   These paints have extremely high visibility and are up to four times brighter than ordinary paints. They glow at night when exposed to light. They are used for safety purposes in and around the home and on all kinds of vehicles, and they are ideal for posters, pop art, and other decorative purposes.

They can be used outdoors and in. They will, however, fade more rapidly on exterior work than ordinary paints and therefore require more frequent recoating to maintain their visibility.

Fluorescent paints are available in latex, alkyd enamel, acrylic lacquer, spray cans, and water colors. The lacquers are designed primarily for industrial use, but the other types lend themselves to home application. The most common color is orange, but yellow, green, blue, red, pink, etc. are sold.

Basic preparation for fluorescent finishes is the same as for ordinary paints. The surface should be clean and smooth. Cover it with the primer recommended by the paint manufacturer. A white rather than dark primer is usually used to make the fluorescent paint stand out most prominently.

Apply fluorescent paint with a soft varnish-brush. Use short strokes to produce an even, rather thick layer. If the paint is applied too thin, there will be streaks and premature fading. Let the first coat dry according to directions on the can before applying a second coat. When the latter is dry, a clear overcoat is applied over an alkyd-base paint.

If you use a latex paint, one coat is usually satisfactory for interior work, but two coats should be used outdoors.

Gloss paints Gloss paints are very shiny and for that reason are rarely used on large surfaces. However, they are practical in that they are hard, somewhat more resistant to scratching than paints with a duller finish, and are by far the easiest to wash. Most gloss paints have a solvent base. Recently a gloss latex has been introduced.

Linseed oil A drying oil made from the seed of flax, it is used mainly as a vehicle in paints and primers, but is also used in furniture finishing.

Raw linseed oil is the oil in its almost pure form. Boiled linseed oil has been heated and contains some added elements. The raw oil penetrates wood more quickly than the boiled, but the boiled produces a richer color when used as a wood finish.

Luminous paints These are phosphorescent paints that are used on objects that must be seen in the dark, such as switch plates and doorknobs. They can be applied by brush or aerosol spray to clean surfaces.

Masonry sealers Clear phenolic, alkyd, epoxy, or urethane sealers are often used on masonry surfaces to minimize staining and make for easier sweeping or washing. They are also used on weathered surfaces to stabilize them.

The sealers are frequently used alone, as on brick paving and marble floors. They may also serve as a primer under other finishes. If used under latex paint, they should be thinned so that they will dry to a low gloss.

Metallic paints These are made with metallic particles—commonly aluminum—suspended in an oil vehicle. They are used for decorative purposes, as sealers, and to reflect heat. Apply with a brush, spray gun, or aerosol.

Miracle coatings There is not a proper name for these materials but you see them advertised frequently in newspapers and almost invariably the word "miracle" is used to describe them. The ad then goes on to explain that these are "space-age" coatings that not only color and protect the outside of your house for a lifetime but also insulate and fireproof it. Also according to advertisements, application is always made by "experts" which make this "miracle" product unavailable to the do-it-yourself painter.

The truth is that the coatings are an ordinary kind of plastic and have no miracle qualities whatsoever. Once applied, they may soon begin to peel off, leaving the house in a mess because when you then try to complete the job of removing all the old coating so that a new finish can be applied, you find it almost impossible to do so short of sandblasting.

These so-called miracle coatings are an expensive gyp. Beware of them.

Multi-color paints These are special paints that contain two or more colors and are used to give two-tone effects on walls and furniture. Most of the paints must be applied with a sprayer, but there are a few available for application by brush. The random color pattern helps conceal small imperfections in the surface.

Odorless paints Solvent-thinned paints that have practically no odor are widely available today. They must, however, be thinned with a special, odorless thinner if they are to stay odorless. If turpentine is used, for example, there will be a "painty" odor. Water-thinned emulsion paints, such as latex, have no odor.

One thing you must bear in mind about odorless paints is that, even though you cannot smell them, they can knock you out just as well as any other paint. Don't use them in a poorly ventilated area.

Plastic paint A term often used to describe almost any kind of paint or finish that contains synthetic rather than natural resins or that contains one of the common plastics, such as vinyl or acrylic. The term is also sometimes applied to thick-bodied paints, such as textured finishes.

Portland-cement paints Portland-cement paints are good for basement and exterior walls and can also be used for concrete swimming pools. They are not suitable for floors, walks, or drives because they lack resistance to abrasion.

The paints contain a high percentage of Portland cement, along with pigments that are not damaged by moisture or the alkali present in masonry. They are inexpensive and, when properly applied, will bond with a masonry surface so they will not blister or peel.

The paint should be applied only to clean masonry or masonry that has been previously coated with Portland-cement paint. Do not use it over any other paint.

The surface should be damp when the paint is applied to make a strong bond. Scrub the paint into the pores of the masonry with a fiber scrub-brush. As soon as the paint has set, sprinkle the surface with a fine water-spray and keep it damp for about 48 hours.

Two coats are needed on new work. The second is applied like the first.

Red lead   Red lead is the oldest and best primer for steel and iron. For best results it should be applied to clean, bare metal. Other primers are available for application over light coats of rust. After the primer is brushed on, it should be overcoated very soon with the final, appropriate finish.

Sanded paints   These are interior latex paints containing fine sand, which gives them a sandy texture when dry. They are used mainly on gypsum-board ceilings and walls to conceal the joints, but can also be used on other imperfect surfaces, wallpaper being the exception.

Sanded paints are best applied with a special texturing brush. Use semi-circular strokes.

There are also sanded paints designed especially for use on diving boards and decks. It is also possible to add fine, dry sand to any conventional deck paint to make it skidproof.

Semi-gloss paints   Semi-gloss paints and enamels are the usual choice for the woodwork in the house and also for walls and ceilings in kitchens and bathrooms because they are more washable than flat paints and less shiny than gloss paints.

Solvent-thinned rubber-base paints   Also known as chlorinated rubber paints, these are excellent for many masonry surfaces. They are highly resistant to moisture and abrasion and make excellent finishes for concrete floors and swimming pools. They are also most suitable for use on cinder, or slag blocks (where latex paints may cause rust stains), and on asbestos cement-board and shingles. An alkyd primer is required when they are used on asbestos cement materials.

The paints are applied with brush, roller, or spray gun.

Textured paints Thick-bodied paints used on interior walls and ceilings, these are available in latex or oil base. There are also powders that can be added to some paints to produce a textured finish. In addition to producing textured effects, the paints are used extensively to cover imperfections in plaster and gypsum-board walls.

Textured paint is applied with a brush. While the surface is wet, make the pattern by going over the wall with crumpled newspaper, a sponge, whisk broom, comb or any other article that will produce a pattern. There are also special rollers for texturing paint.

Textured finishes can be applied over any clean, dry surface.

Tile-like coatings This is the name sometimes given to paints made of a combination of epoxy and polyamide resins. The paints form a very hard, durable, glossy finish, which resembles that of ceramic tile. *See* epoxy paints.

Urethane enamels These enamels are available in one-package and two-package forms. The latter have extremely high adhesion and resistance to abrasion, water, and solvents. Surface preparation and application are the same as for epoxy paints.

Urethane is also used to make a very durable varnish.

Vinyl resins Used in some types of latex emulsion paints, these resins are highly resistant to water, acid, and alkali. Primers made with the resins are often used on metal.

White lead One of the oldest and commonest paint pigments, white lead is still used extensively in exterior paints. It is not used in interior paints because of the health hazard.

White lead mixed with linseed oil is also available in cans. This is thinned with turpentine to produce a paste that is excellent for filling small cracks in wood and for bedding canvas on decks.

Whitewash Composed of lime and other ingredients mixed with water, whitewash was once a common, inexpensive finish, but it has been replaced by more durable water paints, such as latex. A basic whitewash is made with 12 pounds salt, 6 pounds powdered alum, 1 quart molasses, and 8 gallons lime-paste. Thin with water as necessary.

Zinc chromate   Zinc chromate is a metallic pigment used to make zinc chromate primer, the best primer for use on aluminum. This primer is also sometimes used on steel, especially when a light-colored finish is to be applied.

Zinc dust   A metallic pigment used in the primer, which is applied to galvanized steel.

brushes, rollers, painting equipment, and supplies

Besides the necessary amount of paint, you will also need a good deal of other equipment to handle the average paint job. Besides tools used to apply paint—brushes, rollers, spray guns—some or all of the following items are essential on most jobs.

1. Solvent, or thinner, for cleaning equipment and surfaces to be painted.
2. Ladder, stepladder, or scaffolding
3. Drop cloth
4. Mixing pail and paddle
5. Sandpaper, steel or bronze wool
6. Cleaning rags
7. Putty or spackle
8. Putty knife
9. Wire brush

Paint and hardware stores usually stock a wide variety of painting aids—hooks to hang paint cans on ladders, brackets to fasten paint roller pans to ladders, specialized applicators, strainers for paint, and so forth. Most of these products can save you time and effort and are usually worth considering.

PAINT BRUSHES When you buy paint brushes, don't economize! An inexpensive brush is a poor brush that will cause you nothing but trouble. Top-quality brushes are expensive, but they more than pay for themselves through performance.

To begin with, a really good brush has more bristles, holds paint better, and applies paint more smoothly. The bristles have elasticity, yet stay in place. When you press them on a surface, they don't fan out excessively, and when you release the pressure, they spring back into proper position. Furthermore, the bristles don't pop loose from the ferrule. True, even the best paint brush will lose a few bristles, especially when it is new, but the loss is never troublesome.

Whether natural hog-bristles, nylon bristles, or the still-newer polyester bristles are the best is a question for which there is no simple answer. Every painter has his own opinion. The fact of the matter is that they are all good. But watch out for horsehair and oxhair.

TYPES OF BRUSHES   Many types of paint brushes are available. Some are designed for very specific purposes, such as painting radiators, applying calcimine, or stenciling, but the brushes used by most painters are fairly interchangeable, even though they may be known by different names.

Wall brushes are large, flat, rectangular brushes with rather short handles. The most popular sizes are 3 to 5 inches wide.

Trim brushes are 1 to 3 inches wide and are designed especially for use on window frames, baseboards, and other narrow surfaces.

Varnish brushes—the best for applying varnish—are about the same size as trim brushes but have somewhat longer, softer bristles. The brush has a square tip that is cut to a chisel edge on both sides.

Sash brushes, also known as sash tools, are ½ to 1½ inches wide. Some brushes are oval, some flat; some have a chisel-cut tip and some are angular. The handles are long and slender.

As a general rule the best of these four types of brushes have bristles that are at least a half-inch longer than the brush is wide.

DISPOSABLE BRUSHES   Made of plastic sponge mounted on a handle, these can be used with most paints, but not with shellac or lacquer.

HOW TO USE A PAINT BRUSH   Dip a brush to only half its length in the paint; remove the excess paint by tapping the end of the brush against the inside of the can. (If the brush is overloaded, it will drip and splatter when you apply the paint, and the paint film may be so thick that it sags.) Don't drag the brush across the rim of the can.

Hold the brush in whatever way you find most comfortable.

Brush paint on the surface with rather short strokes and then smooth it out with long strokes. Work with the grain. For a very

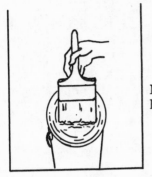

Never dip a brush more than half the length of the bristles into the paint.

Do not remove excess paint from a brush by drawing the bristles edgewise across the can.

The correct way to remove excess paint is to tap the brush against the inside of the can.

smooth finish that doesn't show bristle marks, apply the paint with the grain; smooth it out across the grain, and finish with the grain. The smoothing is done with a brush that is quite dry.

On porous surfaces, brush paint in well. Enamel, varnish, and especially lacquer, however, are applied with a fairly full brush and flowed on.

If you notice thin spots in paint that has begun to set, let it dry before you fill them in.

To avoid ruining a brush, don't use a wide brush to paint a slender object, such as a pipe; and don't try to paint both sides of an inside or outside corner while holding the brush at right angles to the corner. Above all, never jab with a brush.

Don't use a wide brush to paint pipes, railings, and similar surfaces. This will cause the bristles to "fishtail."

If a brush is allowed to stand on its painting tip for any length of time, the weight causes the edge to bend and curl. This will ruin the brush for fine work.

"Fingering" of the bristles is the result of using the narrow edge of the brush in painting. It also occurs if the brush is not thoroughly cleaned after use, causing paint to harden in the heel of the bristles.

HOW TO CLEAN A BRUSH   After use, clean a brush by working it up and down in a can filled with the appropriate thinner. Work the paint out of the bristles just below the ferrule with your fingers. Use a dull knife to take it off the ferrule.

If you intend to continue painting the next day, dry the brush by stroking it back and forth across a newspaper; then set it aside. There is no need to wrap or clean it further.

If you are through painting, however, brush the excess thinner out on newspaper and wash the brush in household detergent solution. Then rinse, brush across newspaper to get it as dry as possible, and let the brush air-dry.

A good way to store brushes while drying or afterwards is to drill a hole through the handle and hang them from a stiff wire. The alternative is to store them flat, in a drawer or box. Wrapping the bristles in aluminum foil or kraft paper helps to protect them.

When it comes time again to use a brush that has been stored, work the bristles back and forth in your hand to remove dirt and loose bristles.

HOW TO SALVAGE AN OLD PAINT BRUSH Fill a can with prepared paint-brush cleaner, which is stronger than ordinary paint thinners. Drill a hole through the handle of the brush, insert a wire, and suspend the brush in the cleaner. The bristles should not touch the bottom of the can. (Never, never let a brush stand on its bristles, since they soon become warped out of shape.)

After the brush has soaked for several hours you can start working the paint out of the bristles with a dull putty knife and an old comb. Continue alternate soaking and cleaning until the bristles are free. Then wash in a rather strong household detergent solution, rinse, and dry.

Paint pads Paint pads are sometimes used instead of brushes for painting sides and other surfaces that do not need to be smoothed out too carefully. The pads are held flat against the painted surface and pulled across it. Their principal advantage is that they hold more paint than a brush of comparable width because they are made of urethane foam with a nylon face and measure up to 4 by 7 inches.

Small, low-piled pads are also available to amateurs who find it difficult to paint accurate, straight lines with brushes.

Paint stripers A paint striper is a handy little gadget for painting lines. It consists of a small bottle, which holds the paint, and a metal head with a revolving wheel, which paints the line.

You can change the width of the stripe simply by changing wheels. You can also paint parallel stripes by putting two wheels on the bottle.

If you want a wider stripe than you can get with a paint striper, draw very light, parallel pencil or chalk lines to mark the edges of the stripe; and a paste masking tape along these. Then just brush paint on the exposed surface.

An excellent way to store a brush after cleaning is to wrap the bristles (be certain that they are straight) in aluminum foil or kraft paper.

Flex the bristles after a brush has soaked for a time in a paint-brush cleaning solution to speed the cleaning action.

Use a dull knife to remove the softened paint from the base of the bristles.

Remove paint from the bristles with an old comb.

Painter's mitt. This mitt is made of the same material as a paint roller and is lined with polyethylene. The mitt is slipped on, dipped into the paint, and wiped on the surface.

Mitts are very handy in cases where it is difficult to get to all sides of the surface being painted, such as railings or walls behind radiators and pipes. They can be cleaned after use in the same way as a paint roller, but don't let the thinner get inside.

PAINT ROLLERS Rollers are highly efficient tools for applying almost every kind of paint and finish to a variety of surfaces. Besides the familiar roller used for painting large flat surfaces, special rollers are available for painting pipes, corners of walls, fences, and even barbed wire. Extension handles permit you to paint ceilings without a stepladder.

It is important to choose the proper roller for the job. For smooth surfaces, such as walls and woodwork, use a roller with a short nap. For sand-finish plaster and gypsum board, a ⅜-inch nap is best. For stucco, smooth concrete, rough plaster, and rough wood-siding, use a ¾-inch nap. And for rough masonry block, use a 1¼-inch nap.

The fabric on the roller cover should suit the type of paint to be applied. Lamb's-wool rollers are fine with oil-based paints, but should not be used with water-thinned latex paints because water softens and swells them. Mohair rollers can be used with any kind of interior flat paint but are recommended especially for applying enamel and all other smooth finishes. Roller covers made from synthetic fibers can be used with all paints, inside and out.

As is the case with paint brushes, it is wise to buy quality rollers. Inexpensive ones should not be expected to turn out first-rate work, and they do not last. A good roller is easy to take apart for cleaning or replacement of the cover and should last for years.

A 7- or 9-inch roller is the best size for most large surfaces. For doors, trim, and other woodwork use a 3-inch roller.

It's a good idea to have several covers for a roller, especially if both oil and water paints are to be applied or if different surface textures are to be painted.

USING A ROLLER Before you begin painting with a large roller, cover edges, corners, and other hard-to-reach areas with a brush, corner roller, or edging roller.

Fill the paint tray to about two-thirds of its maximum depth. Lay the roller into the tray and roll it back and forth over the slanting corrugated section. This will distribute the paint evenly over the entire surface of the roller and remove any excess paint. If the roller drips when lifted from the tray, it is overloaded.

When painting a wall make your first stroke upward. This will keep paint from dripping off the roller. Follow with a down stroke over the same area and then roll cross-wise to get even coverage. As the work progresses, start in a dry area and roll toward one just painted, blending in the laps.

Do not roll so fast that the roller spins and splatters. Feather out the final stroke by using lighter pressure, stopping the roller before lifting it off the surface.

When painting a ceiling, use an extension handle. Work across the width of the room so you can apply a second strip (about two feet wide) before the first gets tacky. Roll the first stroke away from you, slowing down as you reach the wall. A cardboard disk around the handle of the roller helps to guard against paint dripping down the handle on to your hand.

CLEANING ROLLERS A roller used with water-base paint is cleaned with water. Run the roller over old newspapers to remove as much of the paint as possible; then hold it under a running faucet or hose. Another good way to get out paint is to roll the roller back and forth in the paint tray or in a bathtub under a running stream.

Rollers used with solvent-thinned paints should be cleaned with mineral spirits or turpentine. Remove the excess paint on old newspapers; take the cover off the roller; place it in a wide-mouthed jar filled with solvent and shake it a few times. Wipe the roller dry and cover it with aluminum foil or plastic.

PAINT SPRAYERS

PAINT SPRAYERS Spraying is a fast way to paint large wall areas, provided you don't have to spend too much time setting up the spray equipment and masking windows and other surfaces that should not be painted. Spraying is also the ideal way to paint fairly intricate objects, such as fences and wicker chairs, especially if the work can be done outdoors. Finally, spraying is the best and easiest way to produce a flat, textureless paint-surface.

SPRAY EQUIPMENT Some vacuum cleaners are sold with small suction-feed spray guns, but the quality of the work these turn out is uneven and generally rather poor. If you want to enjoy all the advantages of spray painting, rent or buy equipment made specifically for the painter. This consists of a small, portable, electrically driven compressor, a length of hose, a spray gun with an attached cup for holding a small quantity of paint, and, perhaps, a tank for holding a large quantity of paint.

Spray guns used in the home operate in three ways. (1) Suction-feed guns are best suited to small jobs and the application of rather thin materials, such as lacquer, stain, and synthetic enamels. (2) Pressure-feed guns are best suited to application of heavier paints and for larger jobs. (3) All-purpose guns can be converted from suction to pressure feed, which means that if you are going to buy a sprayer, this is the kind to get.

The spray pattern produced by any of these guns varies with the size of the gun and adjustment of the nozzle. Some guns produce a pattern up to 7 inches wide; others produce a pattern up to 14 inches. In all cases the pattern can be adjusted from round to oval. The wide, round pattern is best for spraying large surfaces, such as walls. The oval pattern is used for spraying small or narrow surfaces

SETTING UP TO SPRAY   This is a job you must not slight.

Remove or cover all surfaces that you don't want to paint. If you cover them, make sure they are completely covered because paint spray has an amazing ability to find its way through tiny cracks and holes.

Ventilate the area in which you are painting. Obviously, you don't want a breeze blowing through; but you do want plenty of air to reduce the hazard of explosion. Place the compressor as far away as possible from the spray gun. Have a fire extinguisher handy.

Wear a mask or, better, a respirator, a cap that covers all of your hair, and gloves.

Strain the paint from the can into the sprayer through several layers of cheesecloth or a nylon-mesh stocking.

Practice spraying on sheets of newspaper to make sure the nozzle adjustment is correct and the paint is the right consistency.

HOW TO USE A SPRAY GUN   A spray gun should be held as nearly upright as possible and perpendicular to the surface being painted. When painting a horizontal, flat surface, you may have to tilt the gun somewhat; but if it is feasible to do so, you should try to tilt the surface instead.

Hold the nozzle of the spray gun 6 to 8 inches from the surface and move it back and forth or up and down parallel to the surface. Never arc a stroke, since this produces a paint film of uneven thickness.

When painting across a fairly large surface, spray a vertical

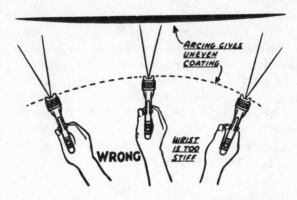

Incorrect method of using a spray gun.

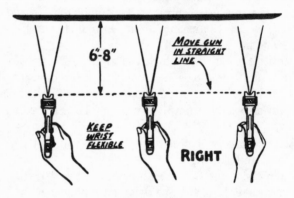

Correct method of using a spray gun.

band at each end; then spray back and forth across the surface. Start each stroke off the work; pull the trigger the instant the nozzle reaches the edge of the work; release the trigger at the other edge of the work, but continue the stroke slightly after this. Called triggering, this technique is necessary to assure that you cover the exact edges of the work without overspraying.

The spray pattern on each stroke should overlap one half of the pattern on the previous stroke.

When painting a long wall you can use up and down strokes, but you will do a better job if you work crosswise. The best way to do this is to paint the wall in 3-foot-wide vertical sections. Overlap the edges of each section by 4 inches.

When painting an outside corner, aim the gun so you spray the surfaces on both sides of the corner at the same time. You can spray inside corners in the same way, but this produces a somewhat uneven film. It is better practice to spray each side of the corner separately.

When painting slender objects, such as balusters in a stair railing, adjust the nozzle so that the spray pattern is just slightly wider than the object.

On open work, such as picket fences and chain-link fences, hold the spray gun at a sharp angle to the work (but don't tilt it up or down) so that the least possible paint will squirt through the openings and be wasted. A good trick, if you can manage it, is to hold a piece of cardboard behind the work so that some of the paint escaping through the openings will bounce back on the work.

CLEANING A SPRAY GUN As soon as you finish painting, clean the equipment. The first step is to loosen the air cap on the gun, while holding a cloth over it tightly and pressing the trigger. This forces paint out of the gun into the paint cup or tank, which is then emptied. Then you spray the appropriate solvent through the spray gun until it comes out clear. Finally, clean off the outside of the gun and the rest of the spray equipment with a cloth soaked in solvent.

ABRASIVES

The painter uses abrasive materials to smooth rough surfaces, to roughen very smooth surfaces, and to remove undesirable or unwanted surface coatings.

His choice of abrasive depends on what he aims to do and on the surface on which he is working. No single abrasive is good for all jobs. Some, in fact, have rather limited usefulness. On the other hand, some abrasives are useful for many things.

A cardinal rule for using abrasives of any kind to smooth wood or a clear finish is to work with the grain, never across it. On other materials that are to be given a clear finish you should go back and forth in the same direction in order to achieve a uniform appearance.

Bronze wool This is similar to steel wool except that it is made out of bronze cuttings and is considerably more expensive. Available in several grades, it is the only kind of metal wool that should be used on boats and other items that are exposed to water. When steel wool is used on such surfaces, small particles that become imbedded in the surface are likely to rust and stain the finish.

Bronze wool should also be used on wood that is to be finished with a water stain.

Sandpaper Three types of sandpaper are in general use by painters and furniture finishers.

(1) Flint paper is the common, garden-variety type of sandpaper. It is surfaced with silica, is pale brown in color, and is cheaper than other papers.

(2) Production paper has a tough aluminum-oxide grit. It costs considerably more than flint paper but lasts much longer and cuts much faster.

(3) Silicon-carbide paper is also known as garnet paper, or waterproof paper. It can be used wet or dry. It is especially good for fine finishing work.

Sandpaper comes in a great many grades ranging from No. 16 (coarsest) to No. 600 (very fine). Nos. 16 through 40 are lumped under the general heading of "coarse"; Nos. 50 through 100 are "medium"; Nos. 120 through 240 are "fine"; Nos. 280 through 320 are "very fine"; Nos. 360 through 600 are called "polishing" papers.

If you don't want to load up on a lot of different grades, a good, basic selection of sandpapers would include Nos. 30, 60, 100 and 150.

The best way to buy sandpaper is in 9- x 11-inch sheets. These are easy to tear along a straight-edge to any size you like.

HOW TO SAND You will get much better results from sanding if you follow a few basic rules:

1. Don't use a coarser sandpaper than necessary. Paper with a large grit doesn't necessarily work any faster than one with a smaller grit, and it may do more damage than good by scarifying the surface unnecessarily. It is especially hard on damp wood.

2. Except when sanding a very slick, hard surface in order to make paint adhere better, always sand wood and plywood with the grain. All other materials should be sanded only in one direction to give a uniform appearance.

3. Don't sand a surface too hard in one spot that is covered with paint, varnish, or other finish: the heat produced will cause the finish to soften and come off. The sandpaper will clog, too.

4. Sandpaper is usually used dry. This produces the fastest cutting action. When sanding paint and other finishes, however, you will help to prevent scratching if you use a waterproof sandpaper and either dip it in water or sprinkle the surface with soapy water.

5. To insure that sandpaper will rub all areas of a surface evenly, wrap it around a block of wood. Use a flat block when sanding a flat surface and a rounded block when sanding rounded surfaces. The ideal flat block has a ¼-inch pad of foam rubber or urethane tacked to the underside.

You should hold sandpaper in your hand and press it down with your fingers only when doing fairly rough work.

6. Maintain even pressure on all parts of the surface being sanded if you want an even finish. Be especially careful not to sand harder at the edges of table tops and the like than in the center.

Sanders   An electric sander is the ideal tool for major sanding jobs on flat surfaces. But the problem is that no single kind of sander is perfect for all jobs; so unless you maintain a well-equipped workshop, it makes sense to rent sanders as you need them.

Disc sanders are in widest use mainly because most electric drills are sold with sanding wheels. However, there are also disc sanders made strictly for sanding and polishing. No matter what the design, this type of sander should be used only for rough work because it has an aggressive action and makes circular scratch patterns.

Belt sanders should not be used for finishing work either because they cut very fast; but they are excellent for taking off tough finishes and working down flat, wood surfaces. The continuous belt rotates in the same way that the tracks on an army tank work.

Orbital sanders make a circular scratch pattern but are somewhat less aggressive than disc sanders and easier to control. They are used for preliminary sanding operations when you are refinishing furniture, wood paneling, wood trim, and built-ins.

Straight-line, or reciprocating, sanders can be used for rough sanding but are particularly suited for finishing work because of their rather gentle action.

Dual-action sanders operate either as orbital or straight-line sanders.

Whatever sander you use, remember that it cuts much faster than you can cut by hand. So it is important to hold it flat and to keep it moving constantly. If holding in one place for any time, it will rapidly chew a hole in the surface. Straight-line and belt sanders must be moved with the grain.

Despite the excellent job that you can do with a straight-line sander, final smoothing of wood that is to be given a fine finish must be done by hand.

Liquid sandpaper This is a special solvent-cleaner made for washing and deglossing paint and other finishes so the new finish will adhere properly. It does this job well, but don't expect it to take the place of sandpaper for other kinds of jobs.

Before using liquid sandpaper on varnish, test it on a small area to make sure it does not dissolve the varnish. It may also soften and remove other finishes if applied too heavily. Just dampen a cloth with it and rub the surface vigorously.

Because this is one of the most toxic materials used by painters, be sure to use it only in a very well-ventilated area.

Emery cloth Emery cloth resembles sandpaper but is made of a sturdy fabric covered on one side with grit derived from a mineral called emery. The cloth is used primarily for cleaning metal and sanding rounded and intricate surfaces that sandpaper does not conform to.

Fine, medium, and coarse grades of emery cloth are available. They are used dry or with oil.

Steel wool Steel wool is used to achieve a very smooth surface on bare wood; to rub down clear finishes; to clean metal and other hard materials; and to wipe off paint and other finishes softened by chemical paint removers. It is ideal for working on rounded and sculptured surfaces because it conforms to the surface and gets into crevices you cannot reach with sandpaper.

The finest steel wool is No. 0000; the coarsest, No. 3.

Although steel wool lacks the cutting power of medium and coarse sandpaper, you should always rub it with the grain of wood or back and forth in the same direction on metal. For smoothing wood and rubbing down finishes, use it dry; for cleaning you can use it with any nonflammable solvent. After finishing a job, wipe off the dust and fragments of steel with a damp cloth, making sure you do a thorough job—especially if you intend to apply a water-based finish—because any particles of steel that are left will rust.

To keep steel fragments from sticking into your skin, wear gloves when you work. And to keep the fragments out of your eyes, don't clean off a surface you have sanded by blowing on it.

OTHER EQUIPMENT   It will be helpful to consider other materials you will need for painting.

Ladders and stepladders Ladders and stepladders suitable for almost every painting need can be purchased or rented. They are available in wood, aluminum, or magnesium. Wood ladders are the heaviest, and the very high ones are extremely difficult for one person to handle alone. Aluminum ladders are considerably lighter, and magnesium ladders, while the most expensive, are the lightest of all—so light, in fact, that more than one person has been stranded on a roof because he failed to secure the ladder, and a gust of wind blew it down.

The most practical kind of ladder for exterior painting is the extension type, which comes in two sections fitted together so that it can be adjusted for varying heights. These are usually available in lengths from 16 to 40 feet. However, in figuring the length of ladder you need, you must allow for a three-foot overlap between the two sections. In other words, if the total stated length of the two sections is 16 feet, the maximum working height of the ladder is 13 feet.

Ladders are priced by the foot, so it is smart to buy the shortest one that will suit your needs. A ladder should be set one-quarter of the length being used from the base of the house. (That is, if you are using 12 feet of ladder, the bottom should be set three feet out from the house.) A ladder should also be high enough so it extends three feet above the highest point that you might be working. This is for safety as well as comfort, because most people find working from a ladder is most comfortable when the top rung is at shoulder height.

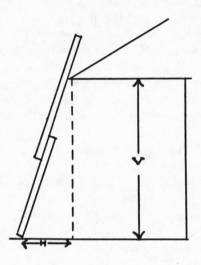

Base of ladder should always be placed so that the horizontal distance (H) is one quarter the distance from ground to eave (V).

The chart below gives some ladder lengths based on heights to eaves:

Height to eaves (feet)	Length of ladder required (feet)
Up to 9½	16
9½–13½	20
13½–17½	24
17½–21½	28
21½–25	32
25–29	36
29–32	40

A good quality metal-ladder should have non-slip adjustable feet and end caps at the top so that it will not damage the painted surfaces it rests against.

Wood ladders should never be painted, because a coat of

paint on the rungs is not only slippery but also will eventually crack and allow moisture to get at the wood and start decay. Treat a wood ladder with a clear wood preservative or penetrating sealer.

WORKING ON A LADDER   First, make sure the ladder is properly placed. As noted above, set the bottom one-quarter of the working height from the base of the wall. Be sure that the rails are resting on a solid, level, non-skid base. If there are any doubts about the surface on which it is resting, secure it by running a rope from the bottom rung to some solid object, such as a tree or shrub, in front of the ladder. Or you can place a boulder or sack of sand behind the ladder.

Never place a ladder in front of a door unless you make certain that the door is locked so no one can open it suddenly and knock the ladder down. Never place a ladder against a window sash. If it is necessary to put a ladder in this location, tie across the top of the rails a wide board that is long enough to extend across the trim on both sides of the window. Thus the ladder will rest on the window frame, not on the sash. (A special device known as a stand-off ladder stabilizer can also be used. The great advantage of this bow-shaped device is that it holds the ladder out from the wall about a foot. Thus you can more easily paint the area behind it.)

Be sure that the locks of the extension ladder are properly secured.

Always climb up and down facing the ladder; and never go so high that the top rung is below the shoulder. Keep both feet on the ladder; and never reach so far that you are off balance. Work from left to right. It's easier to move a ladder than to fall off one. Always keep one hand free to hold on to the ladder with.

There are numerous accessories available that make it easier to work on a ladder more safely. There are safety steps that can be attached to the rungs to give you a wider and more comfortable foot rest, and there are metal trays that can be hung on a rung or attached to the side to hold paint, brush, rollers and paint tray, paint cloths, etc. This equipment can save a lot of going up and down and will make it easier to keep one hand free.

STEPLADDERS   These come in various heights and are made of the same materials as extension ladders. For most home paint-ers, a 5- or 6-foot ladder is most useful. Wood ladders are a bit more stable than metal, which have a tendency to "walk," and the steps are less slippery.

There are also unusual two-piece ladders that can be used both as extension ladders and stepladders. One particular ad-vantage these have is that the legs can be adjusted to different heights so you can place them safely on stairs.

While a stepladder is not so hazardous as an extension, don't take chances with it. Open it all the way, so the extension arms are straight. Make sure it is level and on a firm surface. Don't climb above the third step from the top.

Scaffolding   While an extension ladder is adequate for most exterior painting jobs, you may run into a situation where it is advisable to put up scaffolding. This provides a much larger and more comfortable working base than a ladder.

Scaffolding can be rented at nominal cost from tool-rental concerns, paint stores, and building supply houses. Some types are designed to be fastened to the side of the house; others are hung from windows; still others are built up from the ground. Be sure you find out how to install the equipment and work from it, because falling off scaffolding or having it fall down with you is no more fun than falling off a ladder.

Putty   Four kinds of putty may be used by painters.

LINSEED OIL PUTTY   is used for filling holes in wood, especially outdoors, and for setting window panes. It dries to a hard sur-face, but as it comes from the can it is pliable and easily worked with fingers or a putty knife. You can paint over it immediately, although when you use it in windows, you should let it dry for about a fortnight; otherwise you will wrinkle the surface with your paint brush.

Oil putty should not be applied to bare wood, because the wood will soak up too much of the oil. Always prime the wood with paint or linseed oil. If you use linseed-oil paint or linseed oil, you can apply the putty directly to the damp primer.

Once a can of putty is opened, it tends to dry out quite rap-idly, even though you close the lid tight. You can prevent this by covering it with a film of linseed oil, which should be poured off before you use the putty next time. Putty that has dried

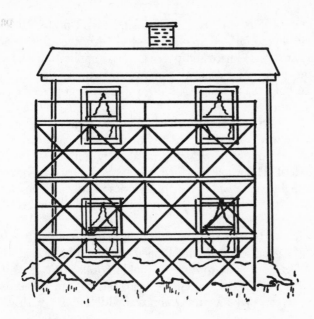

Scaffolding is well worth renting when painting a two-story house, especially if there is a lot of surface preparation to do.

out a little, but not to the point where it is stiff and crumbly, can be reworked by kneading linseed oil into it. However, a new can of putty costs so little that this is hardly worth the effort.

LATEX PUTTY is usually known as elastic putty, because it never completely dries out. It is used mainly for setting window glass and is recommended for this purpose because, if you slam a window or door, the putty absorbs the shock to some extent and helps to keep the glass from breaking. However, the putty hardens so very slowly that, even though you are supposed to be able to paint it within a fortnight, you can do so only if you handle your brush as carefully as if you were working with dynamite.

Latex putty should be applied to wood that has been covered with a primer and allowed to dry. In a tightly shut can, the putty lasts a long time. It should never be reworked if it gets hard.

METAL-SASH PUTTY is a special kind of oil putty made for glazing aluminum and steel windows. It has the same general characteristics as linseed-oil putty as far as application and storage are concerned. Although some manufacturers claim it need not be painted, it should be after it has set for a couple of weeks.

WATER PUTTY —also called wood putty—comes as a dry, plaster-like powder. To use it, mix with water to a workable consistency and apply it with fingers, a putty knife, or any other handy tool. The wood to which it is applied must first be moistened slightly with water. The putty dries rapidly, can be sanded smooth as soon as it is hard, and can be painted within about 12 hours.

Water putty is useful for filling holes and cracks, but it is especially good for repairing chipped edges and holes that other putties will not stick to and for molding into intricate shapes. For example, if a mouse chews away the bottom corner of a door, you can make a strong, almost invisible repair with water putty.

None of the four putties described above should be used in freezing weather.

Caulking In painting, this refers to filling open joints with a material called a caulking compound. Before painting the exterior of a house, it is essential to caulk all joints so that water cannot enter. Much peeling paint, not to mention decay and water damage to inside walls, is due to lack of caulking. Some of the areas that require caulking are: the seams where the siding joins the window and door frames, places where wood joins masonry, and at the base of wood columns and posts. Inside the house, caulking is often required around the rims of bathtubs.

Caulking compound, sold at paint, hardware, and building supply stores, is a mastic that does not get completely hard for a considerable period of time and therefore does not crack as a result of the expansion and contraction of the materials around it. The compound will stick to wood, masonry, and metal and will usually take paint, the exceptions being most silicone caulking-compounds. It comes in several forms, but the best for large jobs in the home is a cartridge that fits into a caulking gun. Small squeeze tubes are useful for little jobs.

Before attempting to caulk a joint, clean it out with a wire

Use a caulking gun to fill all seams in woodwork or where wood joins a different material, such as masonry.

brush. If there are traces of old caulking compound, remove them with a putty knife. The joint must be clean; otherwise the fresh compound will not stick.

If the joint is very wide and deep, pack it first with oakum to within about ½ inch of the surface.

The trick in using a caulking gun is to keep even pressure on the trigger—just enough so that the flow of compound through the nozzle is adequate to fill the joint. Move the gun along at a steady rate with the nozzle pointing forward so it pushes the compound into the joint.

Detergents Any household detergent, except those used for dishwashing and clothes washing, is suitable for removing dirt, grease, oil, and many water-soluble stains from surfaces that are to be painted, stained, or given a clear finish. Household ammonia and washing soda are equally good.

Dilute the detergent according to directions on the label. Rinse cleaned surfaces well with clear water, even though some detergent manufacturers say this is unnecessary.

Drop cloths Drop cloths are used to protect areas, objects, or plants from paint splatters. They are made of light-weight canvas, plastic, or heavy paper impregnated with a waterproofing compound. The last two drop cloths are inexpensive and handy for the occasional painter, but canvas cloths are far superior and worth the investment if you do considerable painting; they last for years. When you spread them out, they hold their position and and are not so easily scuffed up. Most important, they absorb paint splatter; consequently you don't pick up the paint on the soles of your shoes and track it through the house as you do when you use the other kinds of drop cloths.

Old mattress pads also make good drop cloths, although they

are not very large. Newspapers are also usable if you don't have anything else.

Masking tape Masking tape is the amateur painter's friend because it enables him to apply paint exactly where he wants it and not where he doesn't want it. For instance, if you paste masking tape on the floor along the toemold at the bottom of baseboards, you can paint the baseboards and toemold in short order without fear of getting paint on the floor.

Masking tape is also necessary to the professional painter when he is using a spray gun; and he may resort to it when he is brushing paint into hard-to-get-at places.

The glue used on masking tape is designed to hold the tape firmly in place, yet it releases easily when you pull on the tape. It will damage wallpaper but not paint, varnish, or other slick, strong surfaces. And it does not leave a residue, which means you do not have to clean the surface to which it has been stuck before applying a finish.

Metal conditioners Proprietary products, usually containing phosphoric acid and used for treating metal surfaces, such as aluminum, steel, or galvanized steel, before painting. Some conditioners are liquids that are diluted with water; others are jellies. They can be used to remove light rust as well as to etch metal to insure better adhesion of paint.

Muriatic acid Properly called hydrochloric acid, muriatic acid is a poisonous chemical used to clean and etch masonry and metal. Mix it in a plastic pail (never metal). Wear rubber gloves and, if there is danger of splattering, goggles. Apply it with a bristle brush and rinse thoroughly with water as soon as possible afterwards. Avoid breathing in the fumes. Store out of reach of children.

If you get acid on your skin, wash with lots of water and cover the burned area with baking soda. If the acid is taken internally, give liberal doses of ground chalk, raw egg whites, or milk; and call your doctor at once.

Aside from the dangers of muriatic acid, the great problem in using it is to figure out what strength is required. This is because it is sold by hardware and paint stores in a variety of strengths; but unfortunately, the containers rarely indicate what the strength is and the sales clerk doesn't know.

When buying muriatic acid, therefore, shop around until you

find a container that gives complete directions for how it should be diluted and used. If you can't find such a container look for one that contains a 20 percent solution of acid.

A 20 percent acid should be used as is for cleaning and etching dense masonry surfaces and descaling metal. Use it half strength for removing stains from porcelain plumbing fixtures, glazed tile and metal. Use it one-quarter strength for removing efflorescence on masonry.

Oxalic acid Available in crystal form at paint and hardware stores, this acid is diluted with water and used as a bleach for wood. *See* bleaching wood.

Patching plaster Patching plaster is a white powder that is mixed with water to fill holes in plaster and gypsum-board walls and ceilings. It is similar to plaster of Paris but better because it does not set so quickly. Although it can be used instead of spackle for filling small holes and cracks, it is particularly good for repairing large breaks, for which spackle is not suitable.

To fill a hole or crack, open it with a chisel, knife, or similar tool. Try to cut back the edges so that they are wider in back than in front. Blow out all crumbs of plaster. Sprinkle the exposed surfaces lightly with water. Then pack in the patching plaster. When it is dry, sand lightly. The patch will need at least two and perhaps three coats of paint to make it invisible.

In very deep holes the patching plaster should be built up in layers; otherwise it will sag. Fill the hole part way the first time, scratching lines across the plaster so the next layer will adhere well. When the layer has set (it need not be dry), finish filling the hole.

Phosphoric acid This is used for treating rusted metal prior to painting and for etching new metal to insure good paint adhesion. It comes in a concentrate that is diluted with water before use. It is also contained in many commercial metal conditioners.

If you use a concentrate, be sure to follow directions as to the amount of water to be added.

Plastic wood Plastic wood is a mixture of wood fibers and chemicals that is used to fill holes and cracks in wood. It can also be used on other materials. It dries rapidly and, once dry, is resistant to moisture and can be sanded (with some difficulty) and drilled.

The plastic wood sold in most stores is yellow, and should be used only on wood that is to be painted. It does not take a stain when dry, and although you can mix stain with it when wet, you can't be sure you will achieve the desired color. When you intend to use plastic wood under a clear finish, therefore, you should buy a special type that comes mixed with stain. Many colors are available.

Pumice Pumice is a soft stone that is crushed into a fine powder. It is used primarily in furniture finishing to bring a clear finish to a high luster without any objectionable shine. It is also used to clean and dull ceramic tile and other very hard materials before they are painted.

The safest way to use pumice in furniture finishing is to mix some of the powder with vegetable or crude oil in a shallow pan, and then to rub it on the surface with a piece of felt that has first been saturated with oil. For somewhat faster cutting action, you can sprinkle a little pumice on the surface and then rub it with the oil-saturated felt. And for very fast action (but not recommended for amateurs), mix the pumice with water rather than oil.

Whatever method you use, maintain an even, moderate pressure. Rub with the grain. Check the work frequently to make sure you are not cutting too deep. When the job is finally done, wipe the surface clean with a dry cloth or soft paper towels; then go over it with turpentine or benzine to get off all the powder.

For cleaning ceramic tile and the like, pumice is applied with a cloth dipped in water.

Rottenstone An extremely fine powder that is used to achieve the finest luster on furniture with a clear finish. It may also be used to polish metal.

The powder is mixed with a little vegetable oil and then rubbed on the surface—always with the grain—with a piece of felt that is saturated with oil. Do not apply too much pressure. When the desired effect is achieved, remove all traces of the stone and oil with turpentine.

Rottenstone is similar to pumice but softer and less gritty.

Shellac sticks These are pencil-size sticks of dried shellac that are used for making repairs in wood or other hard materials that are given a clear finish. The sticks come in a variety of colors.

To use a stick, heat a small steel spatula over an alcohol flame or on a soldering iron or electric-range burner; hold it on the end of the stick and drip the melting shellac directly into the hole to be filled. Smooth off the shellac in the hole with the hot spatula. Final smoothing can be done with sandpaper or a cloth dipped in denatured alcohol.

Spackle Also called spackling compound, this is a handy type of filler used for small holes and cracks in plaster, wallboard and wood. It can be applied with a putty knife or a finger. There are two forms: one is a dry powder that is mixed with water to make a thick paste; the second, made with vinyl, is ready mixed and can be used just as it comes from the can. Some of the vinyl spackles are fast-drying and can be painted over almost immediately.

Ordinary spackle should not be used for exterior work because it is not waterproof. Use a special spackle made for this purpose.

After spackle has hardened, it can be smoothed with sandpaper. It should then be spot primed so that it will not show up as a dull spot in the final finish.

Swedish putty An old type of wood filler that is little used today. It is made by mixing dry spackle powder with water to form a heavy paste. One-half pound of paste is then mixed with 2½ teaspoons varnish.

Unlike ordinary spackle, Swedish putty is waterproof and can be used outdoors.

Tack rag This is a slightly sticky cloth that is used to pick up every speck of dust and lint on surfaces you are refinishing. It is of particular value when working with varnish.

Prepared tack rags are sold by paint dealers, or you can make your own out of an old sheet cut into a 36-inch square. First wet the cloth in warm water; wring it out lightly; spread it flat and trickle a little turpentine over it. Wring again lightly to spread the turpentine through the cloth; spread flat once more and drizzle about a tablespoon of spar varnish back and forth across it. Wring the cloth hard and shake it to spread the varnish. Let it hang to dry for half an hour or so.

Fold the cloth into a pad by turning the four outer edges in toward the center; then fold in again to make a pad about 9 inches across. The tack rag is now ready for use.

After finishing with the rag on a paint job, shake it out, roll it up and store it in a sealed jar. At any time the rag begins to dry out, you can rejuvenate it with a sprinkle of water, turpentine, and varnish.

Trisodium phosphate This is a strong cleaning agent that leaves no film. It is sold at paint, hardware, and grocery stores under such brand names as Soilax, Spic-and-Span, and Oakite.

Wash primer This is similar to a metal conditioner. It usually contains phosphoric acid and is used to promote adhesion of paint to metal. Wash primers are available in either one- or two-package form.

Water glass Known as sodium silicate, it is used for sealing concrete floors to stop dusting of the concrete. Before using, the floor should be scrubbed clean with detergent solution, rinsed, and allowed to dry. Dilute the water glass with water according to the maker's directions and apply with a mop or hair broom. Brush it into the concrete well and allow 24 hours for drying. Then scrub with fresh water, allow to dry again, and make a second application. A third application is required and made in the same way.

A concrete floor treated with water glass cannot be painted or covered with resilient flooring.

Wax Wax is used not only to protect finishes from scratching, staining, and water spotting but also to give them a soft, easy-to-maintain luster. Solvent-base waxes are applied to wood because they do not raise the grain, as water-base waxes do. The main use for such waxes is on wood floors, but they are also used on wood paneling, woodwork, and furniture that receives hard usage.

A white, liquid wax (with a water base) is applied primarily to kitchen appliances and painted cabinets.

REMOVAL Before you apply paint or clear finish to a surface, all wax and polish must be removed. The best way to do this is to wash the surface with benzine, naphtha, or mineral spirits, and then to scrub it hard with steel wool. (Or you can start with steel wool and then use the solvent.) In an extreme situation, a prepared wax remover made for cleaning resilient floors may prove helpful; but since it can raise wood grain, you may have to sand the surface lightly when it is dry.

Wood fillers *See* plastic wood, putty, shellac sticks, and spackle. These are the principal materials used for filling fairly large holes and cracks in wood.

To fill the pores of open-grained woods, use a paste wood-filler or shellac. *See* fillers.

Wood preservatives   Wood preservatives are chemical compounds used on wood to make it more resistant to decay, fungi, and attack by wood-eating insects, such as termites. The preservatives also help to stabilize the moisture content of wood and thus minimize warping, swelling, and shrinking.

Among the things that can benefit from treatment with a preservative are fences, trellises, wood gutters, window and door frames, and other wood items that are exposed to a lot of moisture or installed near or in contact with the ground.

Wood that has been pressure treated at the factory with a preservative lasts longer than that which is treated by hand at the time of installation. But hand treatment is better than none at all. Application can be made with a brush, roller, or spray gun, but the best method is to dip the wood in preservative for several hours.

If wood is not to be given a finish, the best preservative to use is creosote or pentachlorophenol or copper naphthanate in a heavy oil vehicle. Wood that is to be painted, however, must be treated only with pentachlorophenol or copper naphthanate in a light oil vehicle or with a preservative dissolved in water. Be sure to read the label on the can of preservative to make sure you can paint over it.

Wood that is to be given a clear finish can also be stained, but in this case you should not use copper naphthanate, because it colors the wood green.

Amalgamators   An amalgamator is a special kind of solvent that may be used to restore a badly scratched varnish finish. When brushed on the varnish and allowed to stand, it softens the varnish so that it will flow together to form a smooth surface. After the varnish hardens, let it stand for a couple of days; then rub it with very fine steel wool or pumice to cut the high gloss left by the amalgamator.

paint problems and failures

Good-quality paints and finishes applied to a properly prepared surface in accordance with the manufacturer's directions can be expected to produce good results. When there is a problem or a failure, it is usually not the fault of the paint but the result of improper preparation of the surface, using the wrong type of paint for the material involved, or improper application.

Most paint problems and failures occur on outside work, where the weather takes its toll. The most common and serious ones involve the outside of the house. But failures can also show up on interior work and even furniture.

PROBLEMS   A good paint job on the outside of a house should last four to six years. Paint inside the house should last even longer. If something goes wrong ahead of schedule, it is probably due to one of the following:

Poor-quality paint or the wrong paint for the surface.

Improper application of paint.

Improper surface preparation.

A serious moisture condition.

Natural causes.

Here are the most common paint problems, how you can recognize them, and what you can do about them:

BLISTERING   A paint blister resembles a blister on the hand; it looks like a bubble. Sometimes the paint blisters are few and far between; sometimes they are confined to a small area; sometimes they appear over a wide area. Often if you split one with a knife, the exposed area will be wet. This is because blistering is caused by moisture that has somehow got behind the paint film and pushed it off the wood. In time, the blisters will start to peel.

The remedy for blistering is to find the source of the moisture that is causing trouble and to correct it. Sometimes the water gets in from outside; frequently it comes from inside the house, usually as a result of condensation.

If the blisters are localized around windows, eaves, and cornices, you may assume that rain is reaching the wood by way of some small crack or open seam. Cleaning out all joints and filling them with caulking compound usually corrects the problem.

Blisters around gutters and downspouts often indicate some problem with these units. It may be that the gutters overflow because they are not properly pitched; or that they have become clogged with leaves and other debris. The start of the remedy is to get the gutters and downspouts back into working order so they carry off the water running into them and do not spill it on to painted surfaces.

When blistering is found over a large area, the chances are that the moisture originates inside the house. This is a very common condition today because houses are tightly constructed, and the average household produces a tremendous amount of moisture from clothes dryers, showers, cooking, etc. All of this moisture goes into the air inside the house as a vapor and is drawn to the colder air outside the house. Unless the house is very well ventilated, the moisture vapor passes right through the exterior walls; and when it finally comes into contact with the siding in back of the paint film, it condenses into water. This soaks into the siding and eventually blisters the paint film.

Large areas of blistering are frequently found on those walls enclosing rooms with a high moisture output—the bathrooms and kitchen, for example.

The most effective way to prevent this build-up of moisture is through adequate ventilation. Exhaust fans in the kitchen and each bathroom are extremely desirable. Clothes dryers should be vented directly to the outdoors.

One other thing you should do to reduce the possibility of further blistering is to insulate all walls, the roof, and floors over unheated spaces and to install continuous vapor barriers on the warm side of these surfaces. In a new house, vapor barriers are frequently made with large sheets of polyethylene film. Many insulating batts and blankets have built-in vapor barriers. In an existing house, two coats of alkyd or latex paint or varnish on the inside surfaces of exterior walls, top-story ceilings, and floors over unheated spaces form excellent vapor barriers. Vinyl wall-coverings are also very good.

Problems with blistering can also be corrected by using a latex paint on the outside of the house. Latex is a "breathing" paint, which permits the moisture behind it to escape. The difficulty here is that the paint must be applied to bare wood or masonry. If the latex is applied over an old non-breathing existing paint, the old paint will continue to blister. This means that old, non-breathing paint must be removed. The walls should then be primed with a latex primer, followed by latex house paint.

If you are unable to correct the moisture condition inside the house, removing old exterior paint and applying exterior latex are usually well worth the time, effort, and money involved.

ABNORMAL CHALKING   While normal chalking (see chalking) is a desirable feature of house paints, abnormal chalking is something else again.

Abnormal chalking is often caused by applying paint in such a thin film that rapid disintegration is an almost inevitable consequence. Abnormal chalking can also be due to using only one coat of paint over a porous surface when two coats are required. Home owners often bring this problem on themselves when they apply a paint with good hiding power over a porous surface. Because the old surface is hidden, the tendency is to use one coat instead of two. But what happens is that the binder in the new paint is quickly absorbed by the porous surface, leaving only a thin coat of pigment, which soon begins to wash away.

The obvious remedy for abnormal chalking is another coat or two of paint.

CHECKING AND ALLIGATORING   When paint checks, small interlaced cracks appear over the surface of the topcoat only. The condition results from use of poor-quality paint that does not contain sufficient binder. Before repainting, the area should be scraped or sanded smooth.

Alligatoring is a more advanced form of checking. The surface is so rough that it resembles alligator skin. Since a fresh coat of paint will not hide this condition, the remedy is to take off the paint down to the bare wood and start over again.

CRACKING   Here the paint is cracked right down to the bare wood. It can be due to moisture in the wood, an inferior paint lacking elastic qualities, or a paint that was not properly mixed before application. Cracked paint should be removed completely before you repaint.

CROSS-GRAIN CRACKING   In this situation cracks appear across the grain of the wood. They indicate that too many thick layers of paint have built up and that they are too stiff to accommodate the normal shrinking and swelling of the wood. This often occurs in older houses. The paint must be removed.

CRAWLING   When paint crawls, it draws itself up into bubbles soon after it is applied. The condition may result from applying paint when the weather is too cold or humid. It may also result from poor mixing of the paint or from painting over a greasy or waxy surface. In any event, stop painting until you have determined the cause of the problem.

WRINKLING   Paint is said to wrinkle when it dries with a rough, crinkled texture. The main cause is the application of too thick a coat at one time. What happens is that the top surface will dry, while the underlayer is still soft. Wrinkling may also occur for the same reason if paint is applied to a very cold surface on a fairly warm day with low humidity.

Whatever the cause, the wrinkled paint should be removed before you repaint.

PEELING   Peeling can occur between the topcoat of paint and the next coat down or between the entire paint film and the painted surface.

When the entire paint film peels, a moisture condition similar to that which promotes blistering is usually the cause. Follow the corrective measures given above.

Peeling between paint coats—known as intercoat peeling—may indicate that the undercoat was too greasy or glossy to permit good adhesion. A much less familiar but possibly more widespread cause of this peeling on exterior surfaces is an unreasonable delay between the application of paint coats, particularly between the application of the primer and finish coat.

According to the Forest Products Laboratory, you should not allow more than a 14-day lapse between exterior paint coats.

Whatever the cause of intercoat peeling, the only way to correct it is to remove the peeling coat, sand and clean the undercoat, and then repaint.

SLOW DRYING If paint or other finish does not dry as fast as usual or as fast as the label on the can indicates it should, it may be because the paint is too old; or because you applied it when the temperature was too low or too high; or because of peculiar atmospheric conditions.

Inside a building the problem can sometimes be corrected simply by raising the temperature somewhat. But if a finish continues to remain tacky long after its normal drying period, the best procedure is to remove it with solvent and try again, preferably with a new can of paint. (*See* paint, storage.)

FADING Virtually all pigmented stains and paints except whites will fade. As might be expected, exterior paints fade more than interior; those on the south side of the house fade more than those on the north. Unfortunately, there is nothing you can do to stop this. You can, however, minimize fading if you use the best available paints, because they contain more pigment than cheap paints.

If fading occurs in a clear finish, it is hardly noticeable. But the wood to which the finish is applied often fades drastically. Here again, there is nothing you can do except screen the faded articles from the sun.

DISCOLORING Several things will discolor paint: knots and creosote stains bleeding through the finish; soluble salts in cedar and redwood bleeding through the finish; water dripping over green copper-oxide, rust, or moss, which deposits stains on the finish.

Bleeding of knots and creosote stains can be stopped by priming the bare or painted wood with a stain killer. Staining the finish on cedar and redwood usually stops discoloration naturally; if not, you must take steps to keep moisture from getting into the wood (*see* blistering, above). Copper and rust staining is stopped by priming and painting the metal properly. Moss staining is stopped by killing the moss.

INSECTS It is not at all unusual for a few bugs to get into

fresh paint, but sometimes they can be a real nuisance. This usually occurs when a light is left burning at night near the vicinity of wet paint.

The way to prevent the problem is obvious—don't leave lights burning long enough to attract bugs. This applies to lights inside the house as well as out. For example, if you leave a light burning in a room near a window that opens on to a porch you have just painted, the next morning you will probably find that the paint around the window is peppered with gnats and other night-flying insects.

Chalking Chalking is usually associated with exterior house paints. It is a slow disintegration of the paint film, which produces a powdery substance that will come off on your hands or a cloth rubbed across the surface.

Normal chalking is desirable, especially on a white house, because it helps to keep the painted surface clean. Dirt and soot that settle on the paint are washed off with the chalk when it rains. Chalking is also good because it gradually reduces the thickness of a paint film so that the surface can be painted at normal intervals without building up an excessive thickness of paint.

Chalking paints should be used only on the body of a house and on other outside surfaces, such as fences, where there would be no possibility of the chalk run-off staining a surface that is painted another color. For example, windows, shutters, and other pieces of outside trim that are to be painted a special color should always be painted with a non-chalking, hard-surfaced trim enamel. Chalk-resistant house paints should be used on siding that is in contact with or above masonry that is not painted the color of the siding. The same paint should also be used in regions with heavy rainfall because they last longer than chalking paints.

Abnormal chalking is an undesirable problem discussed elsewhere (*see* paint, problems).

Condensation Water vapor escaping from a house is often responsible for blistering of paint on exterior walls. For how to control this problem, *see* blistering.

Condensation forming on windows in winter also often does considerable damage to the finish on the window frames, muntins, and sills. In very cold climates, even worse damage may be done to paint on the inside of exterior walls. The latter problem defies solution. Condensation on windows can be stopped, however, by installing storm windows. True, you will then get condensation on the storm windows, but the damage done to them is less severe and also less noticeable.

Knots, sealing Knots in softwood that has not been adequately seasoned (that includes most lumber sold today) will bleed through paint—even through several coats. To prevent this, brush orange shellac or pigmented knot-sealer on the knots. Application is best made to new wood but can be made after painting whenever brown stains appear. If you use shellac, two finish-coats of paint will be needed to conceal the glossy spots made by the shellac.

You should note that years of testing by the U.S. Forest Products Laboratory indicate that no ordinary knot sealer, including the two just mentioned, can be guaranteed to stop the bleeding of knots. The only one recommended by the laboratory is known simply as WP-578 knot sealer. This is effective only if applied to bare wood. It follows that if you are painting new wood, you should use this sealer if you can find a paint dealer who sells it. That, unfortunately, is a hard thing to do.

Bleeding stains Stains containing creosote are likely to bleed through any oil or water paint applied over them. Occasionally other types of stain and varnish stain cause the same trouble.

Actually, if an exterior creosote stain has weathered for a year or more, it usually will not bleed, but it's best not to take chances. In fact, unless you know what sort of stain has been used on wood, don't take chances on any of them.

It is very easy and inexpensive to prevent bleeding simply by coating the stained wood with shellac or a pigmented knot-and-stain sealer. Aluminum paint can also be used.

Creosote, painting over Before painting over wood that has been stained or preserved with creosote, a sealer must be applied to keep the creosote from bleeding through. Special stain-kill sealers are available for this purpose. One coat of aluminum paint is also excellent.

Note that creosote that has weathered outdoors for over a

year may not bleed through paint, but there is no assurance that it won't. Hence there is the need for overcoating with some sort of sealer.

Mildew   Mildew is a fungus that attaches itself to painted surfaces and appears as a dark discoloration. It is most common in warm, humid areas but can be a problem almost anywhere in damp parts of the house.

Mildew must be removed before you apply paint. If not, the paint will spread the spores to other areas and the original mildewed spots will show through the paint.

To kill mildew, wash the affected area with a solution of ⅔ cup trisodium phosphate, ⅓ cup household detergent, and 1 quart household chlorine-bleach. Add enough warm water to make a gallon. Scrub the area well and then rinse with fresh water. Wear rubber gloves.

Where mildew is a common problem, it is best to use paints that contain mildewcides. Many other paints (but not all) can be made mildew-resistant by the addition of special fungicides sold in paint stores.

Burned wood   If still sound, wire-brush or sand the burned areas to remove as much of the carbon as possible. Coat with shellac or an alcohol-based pigmented primer before applying the finish coat.

Efflorescence   Efflorescence is a thick, whitish powder that appears on masonry surfaces—primarily brick—as a result of the reaction of moisture with the alkalis in the masonry. It is a particular problem with new masonry surfaces.

If efflorescence is in evidence before masonry is to be painted, it must be removed. Use a weak solution of muriatic acid. Apply this with a bristle brush and scrub hard for about a minute. Then rinse immediately with clear water. Apply paint when the masonry is dry (or while it is still damp if you use latex paint).

Painting masonry does not necessarily prevent further efflorescing, because water may continue to seep into the masonry and react with the alkali salts. But the condition generally subsides after a treatment with acid.

Moss   Moss often grows on roofs, exterior walls, and pavements that are located in damp, shady areas. It is an implacable enemy of painters because it prevents paint from sticking, discolors it, and even grows right through it. Water running over moss stains the surfaces below; and in time the moss itself starts to grow on the stained areas.

Although moss will grow on most exterior building-materials that are not glassy smooth, it is particularly prevalent on wood-shingle roofs and brick walls and pavements. To control it on roofs, brush it off when dry and brush on pentachlorophenol wood-preservative. Scrub other types of roofing with ½ ounce sodium arsenite in 10 gallons water. Take care not to let either of these liquids splatter on plants because they will kill them.

Sodium-arsenite solution can also be used on brick walls and paving. Or you can use Ammate, a garden chemical used to kill undesirable weeds, tree stumps, etc. Scrub the bricks hard in order to work the chemical into the pores. A strong solution of Clorox is sometimes recommended for killing moss, but it is not a sure remedy.

Alkali A soluble mineral-salt present in Portland cement. Because alkali can be harmful to some paints and because almost all masonry contains a certain amount of it, use only alkali-resistant paints on masonry.

how to remove paint

There are several ways you can strip off old paint, varnish, shellac, and other coatings. Which method to use depends on the area involved as well as on the type of finish you are dealing with. It is sometimes necessary to use several methods to achieve results.

HEAT This is one of the easiest, quickest, and least expensive ways to remove heavy accumulations of paint from large surfaces, such as the house walls, a door, the hull of a boat, etc. The paint is not burned off. On the contrary, you apply just enough heat to soften the paint film so it can be scraped off with a putty knife or paint scraper.

Heat is provided by a gasoline blowtorch, propane torch, electric scraper, or infra-red lamp.

One of the chief drawbacks in using heat to remove paint is the danger of fire. Gasoline and propane torches are especially hazardous because there is an open flame. An electric paint scraper is also dangerous because accumulations of paint can build up underneath and eventually burst into flame. On the other hand, although an infra-red lamp is slow, it does not create a fire hazard. It is therefore popular with boat owners because it can be used safely on interior work and also does not produce the dangerous fumes that arise from some types of chemical paint removers.

The other disadvantage of using torches and electric burners is the danger of scorching the wood. This is not a great problem if the surface is to be repainted because the paint will hide any discoloration; but if the wood is to be given a natural finish, you are in for a long, slow bleaching and sanding job. Hence it is wise to remove the paint by other methods.

Heat from any source should never be used to remove finish from furniture because, aside from the risk of scorching the wood, the heat may soften the glue in the joints.

To minimize fire hazard, gasoline and propane torches should be used for exterior work only. Even at that, you should not use them on clapboards or shingles because the flame may get in under the butts and start a fire in the wall cavity.

The wind should be relatively calm in order to permit control of the flame. Don't direct the flame toward window glass. You should also be careful not to use a torch on a surface that has been previously treated with a paint remover, as many of these are inflammable. Keep a garden hose or fire extinguisher handy.

The trick in using a torch is to keep the flame about two inches away from the surface and at a slight upward angle. If you are using a gasoline torch, adjust the flame so it is red rather than blue. Hold the flame at one point until the paint begins to bubble and then move the flame ahead and immediately remove the softened paint with a putty knife or scraper. Keep the flame about two inches ahead of the scraper. It will take a bit of practice before you learn to coordinate the movement of the flame and the putty knife, but you must remove the paint while it is still warm. Once it has cooled, it will not come off easily.

There are paint scraper attachments that you can use with a propane torch, but you will probably need a putty knife anyway.

Electric scrapers are a good deal safer than a torch, but as previously mentioned, they do produce enough heat to set paint on fire. With care, however, they can be used on interior work, and are excellent for exterior work. A heavy-duty extension cord is needed to operate them at a distance from an outlet.

Electric scrapers come with a built-in scraper attachment, but you will also need a putty knife to pick up paint that the attachment misses. To operate a scraper, let the heating element heat up. Then place the scraper over the paint and hold it there until the paint bubbles and can be scraped off. The work goes quite rapidly. Remove paint that accumulates around the heating element from time to time.

Infra-red lamps are used in the same way, except that they do not have a built-in scraper. Hold the lamp in one hand and a putty knife or scraper in the other.

CHEMICAL PAINT AND VARNISH REMOVERS These contain chemicals that soften paint and other finishes so they can be removed with a putty knife, scraper, scrap of burlap, or pad of coarse steel wool. They are the most popular way to remove paint, for they are quick, do a good job and are easy to work with. They can be used on practically every type of surface and finish. Because they are relatively expensive, they are seldom used on large areas, such as house walls, except when it is impractical to use a flame or hand scraper.

Chemical paint removers should be handled with great care. Many are highly toxic, and some are highly inflammable. All contain strong chemicals that can burn the skin. Wear rubber gloves. Goggles are also desirable. Work only in well-ventilated areas.

There are two basic types of paint remover—the liquid and the paste. Liquid removers are the faster and are particularly suited for use on intricate surfaces because they flow into the crevices. On the other hand, they can be used easily only on horizontal surfaces. They contain benzol, which makes them very inflammable and toxic.

The paste remover, a creamy substance, is more popular because it sticks to vertical as well as horizontal surfaces. It is somewhat slower acting, but as a rule is less toxic than the liquid. Some types are non-flammable.

Some paste and liquid removers contain wax, or paraffin, to slow down the evaporation of the solvents. When this kind of remover is used, the wax that remains on the surface must be taken up with turpentine, mineral spirits, or benzine before a new finish is applied. Otherwise, the wax will prevent the new finish from drying properly. Increasing numbers of removers, however, are of the water-wash type. Treated surfaces are simply cleaned with water. There are also a few rather expensive removers that require no rinsing at all.

For average home use, the simple water-wash removers are probably best.

Before using a paint and varnish remover, read the directions on the label. Most require that you shake the container before opening. Unscrew the top slowly and do not hold your face right over it; if the contents are warm, they may splash up when the pressure is relieved. Pour a quantity of the remover into a small, clean container that has not previously been used to mix paint, because the paint would be softened.

It is best to apply paint removers with a brush that has an unfinished handle. If the handle is painted the remover will soften the paint, and this might discolor the surface you are working on.

The trick in using any remover is to let the remover do the work. If there are several coats of paint, several applications of remover may be necessary to remove one coat at a time. If you're working on furniture or other fine work, it is especially important to allow the remover to soften the paint so that it can be easily removed with a putty knife, burlap, or steel wool. If the paint is not completely soft, you may damage the wood as you attempt to remove it.

Liquid removers require a different application technique, in that the remover must be kept wet. This requires continuous applications until the paint is soft.

When using a paste remover, apply a thick coat with short strokes. Brush in one direction and do not go back over the remover, since this disturbs the film that forms on the remover and reduces its efficiency. It generally takes 20 minutes or so for the remover to do its job completely. You can test the condition of the paint by scraping a small area with your putty knife. If it peels off easily, the remover's work is finished.

When paint is taken up with a putty knife, keep scraping the knife off on old newspapers in order to maintain an adequately sharp edge. If you use steel wool or rags, wash them out frequently in detergent solution (if the remover is of the water-wash type). Old toothbrushes, toothpicks, spatulas, and other small tools used to get paint out of carvings, grooves, and other difficult places should also be kept clean.

SANDING   While small areas are often sanded by hand, an electric sander should be used on large areas. Special sanders are used on wood floors. For other jobs, you can use either a vibrating, belt, or rotary sander. For more about these, see sanding.

Actually, sanding is not a popular way to strip a finish from a large area (except a wood floor) because it is rather difficult work. The method is used, however, when heat or paint removers might be dangerous. It is also a good method for rapidly cleaning up large surfaces that are marred by numerous scratches, bumps, chipped, and peeling spots but which also have a good deal of sound paint.

SCRAPING   Dry scraping (without heat or paint remover) is resorted to when it is necessary to take off small amounts of finish in areas that are difficult to get at in other ways. For instance, you would use a scraper to remove floor finish in the corners of a room, paint on window mullions, etc.

The tool known as a scraper is a simple wooden handle with a steel blade clamped to one end. You hold the handle more or less parallel with the surface to be scraped, press the blade on the paint, and pull the scraper toward you. If necessary, you can press down on the handle just above the blade with your other hand to get better traction. The blade must be sharpened frequently with a metal file, stroking it lengthwise along the bottom edge.

Other tools used for scraping are putty knives, pocket knives, and beer-can openers.

SANDBLASTING   This is the only practical way to remove paint from very large masonry surfaces, particularly if the surface is rough or the paint is an epoxy. The work is usually done by professionals at a rather high price. You can, however, rent sandblasting equipment from some tool-rental outlets. The equipment is run by electricity or gasoline and utilizes compressed air to drive the sand against the surface being treated.

how to paint and finish wood

No other material can be finished in so many ways, is so easy to finish, or holds a finish better than wood. And no other material, except steel, needs a finish more to protect it from deterioration.

Regardless of whether the wood you are finishing is used in fine furniture or as rough siding, it must be dry and sound if it is to hold paint. And it must be kept dry if it is to continue to hold paint.

It follows that when you finish a piece of wood for the first time or the tenth time, you must make sure it is not damp. Usually you can tell this by touching it with your fingers or lips. Or you can rub it with fairly coarse sandpaper. If this causes bad scratches and splintering and does not produce a dust, the wood is wet.

If you have any doubts following these tests, or if you know the wood has been exposed to water or high humidity in the past few days (even though it now feels dry), give it plenty of time to dry (48 hours is about the minimum for siding and exterior woodwork that has been rained on). A much longer drying period is needed if you buy obviously wet lumber from a yard or if you have had a serious condensation problem in the house.

Checking wood for decay is a simpler matter because the rot is usually visible or makes the wood feel spongy. Termite damage can be detected by driving an icepick into the wood. If it goes in easily you know that termites have been at work.

Since there is no way to restore decayed or termite-riddled wood to a sound condition, and since paint will not last on unsound wood, you should replace the wood before getting out your paint brush.

PREPARING WOOD FOR PAINTING   The steps to be taken vary with the condition of the wood and what you aim to do, but they will include some of the following:

Fill holes, dents, cracks, and deep scratches. The wood must be primed before certain fillers are applied.

Glue loose knots.

Prime knots with shellac or a knot sealer.

Sand burned spots down to clean wood.

Sand the entire piece of wood to make it smooth.

Remove defective finish.

Apply a bleach to eradicate stains or to change the wood's color.

Fill pores in open-grained wood.

Sand the end-grain smooth or work paste-wood filler into it.

Apply a wood preservative.

FINISHES   Many finishes that can be applied to wood are described elsewhere in this book. The following is a simple, condensed list of those which are especially recommended:

Siding: Alkyd house paint, linseed-oil house paint, latex house paint, pigmented oil-stain. For a clear finish, water repellent.

Trim, doors, windows: Alkyd trim and shutter enamel.

Decks: Pigmented oil-stains designed for decks.

Interior woodwork, walls, windows: Alkyd semi-gloss enamel. For a clear finish, varnish.

Wood paneling: Alkyd semi-gloss enamel. For a clear finish, varnish, shellac, or stain wax.

Floors: Solvent-base floor enamel. For a clear finish, penetrating floor-sealer, urethane varnish.

Furniture: Solvent-base gloss enamel. For a clear finish, furniture varnish, shellac, linseed oil.

Children's furniture and toys: Solvent-base gloss enamel that is free of lead.

If wood is to be given a clear stain use an oil stain, unless the final finish goes on and holds up better over an alcohol or water stain. The stain is applied before pores in the wood are filled. Allow the stain to dry 48 hours or more before applying varnish or other clear finish.

On new wood, paint should always be applied over a compatible primer or undercoater. Pigmented stains and all clear finishes, however, may serve as their own primers, but shellac is often used as a primer under varnish and lacquer.

Cedar   The ideal finish for cedar shingles, shakes, clapboards, and board siding is a clear or pigmented oil-stain. Because of the relative porosity of the wood, the stain penetrates deeply and lasts a long time. By contrast, paint, while wet, tends to flow off the high spots (particularly the ridges on shingles and shakes) and settles in the low spots; consequently, the high spots lose their finish long before the low spots.

The additional advantage of a stain is that it doesn't conceal the attractive texture of cedar, as paint does.

None of this means, however, that you cannot use paint if you prefer it. Latex is recommended because of its breathability.

One other type of finish that has become popular in recent years is bleaching oil. This is a type of stain that contains bleach as well as penetrating oil and a light-gray pigment. The pigment gives cedar an immediate gray color, while the bleaching chemical accelerates the normal weathering process. After six months, cedar treated with this finish looks as naturally weathered as old houses on Cape Cod.

One problem that often arises when cedar siding is coated with a fairly light-colored pigmented stain or paint is the appearance of discolored areas on the surface. These are caused by water-soluble substances within the wood that bleed through the paint film. Normally the bleeding occurs during the first year, and the discolorations are soon weathered away. If they continue to mar the surface, however, the chances are that you have a moisture problem in the walls. For how to cope with this, *see* paint, problems.

Hardboard   Hardboard is made by compressing wood fibers into a thin, dense, very hard panel. Some panels have a very smooth surface on both sides; some on only one side. Ordinary panels are unfinished, but special panels are available with durable baked-on finishes, wood-grain finishes, or prime coats.

Before finish is applied to any hardboard, the panels should be washed with detergent solution and rinsed.

Unfinished hardboard used indoors can be covered with virtually any interior finish, but the best opaque finish is an alkyd interior paint (flat, semi-gloss, or gloss, depending on how the hardboard is used). Apply a primer first, and follow with one or two finish coats. If the rough backside of a panel is painted, it will probably require an additional coat because it is very porous.

For a clear finish on unfinished hardboard, use varnish, shellac, or lacquer. The panels can be stained beforehand with oil stains or with colors-in-oil or flat oil-paint thinned with turpentine. If stain is not used, it is advisable first to apply a wood sealer that is reduced 50 per cent with naphtha or benzine; otherwise the varnish, shellac, or lacquer will darken the surface somewhat.

Hardboard panels with a factory-applied wood grain should be protected with a couple of coats of dull varnish.

Panels with a baked-on finish do not require painting until the enamel is damaged or you want to change the color. At that time, sand scarred enamel to a feather edge and roughen the entire surface slightly. Then apply an alkyd or latex.

Exterior hardboard siding that is factory-primed should be painted according to the maker's directions soon after installation. Generally, because of the extreme density of hardboard, you should use only an oil-base house paint.

Prime unfinished siding with oil-base primer followed by two coats of oil-base house paint.

Hardwoods Hardwoods are called hardwoods because, as opposed to pine, fir and other softwoods, they are generally harder, denser, and heavier. In actual fact, however, some hardwoods are softer and lighter than some softwoods.

Hardwoods are also generally considered to show more variation in the color of the sapwood and heartwood than softwoods. But here again there are exceptions. In basswood and chestnut, for example, the heartwood and sapwood are almost identical in color.

Hardwoods, in other words, are a mixed kettle of fish; and there are not firm rules for finishing them. The following general rules are applicable, however:

1. Never sand or scrape hardwoods across the grain, because the scratches left are much more difficult to eradicate than in softwoods. For the same reason, it is also advisable not to use too coarse a sandpaper, even when sanding with the grain.

2. Bleaching is frequently necessary if you want to achieve a more even color in a hardwood.

3. Because hardwood knots rarely bleed, there is no need to spot-prime them with shellac or a knot-sealer.

4. Hardwoods can be painted like softwoods, but because of the handsome color, grain, and texture of many hardwoods, a natural finish is generally preferred. For the best finishes to apply, *see* furniture, wood. Many special finishes are also described throughout this book.

Particle board Also known as chipboard or flakeboard, particle board is made of wood fragments bonded together to form a hard, smooth, dimensionally stable panel. Because particle board is somewhat porous, it is advisable to apply a paste wood-filler before painting, especially if you want a very smooth surface. Exposed edges of particle board are extremely porous and must also be filled with wood filler or covered with flexible, veneer-thin wood tapes.

Whether you intend to apply a clear or opaque finish, prime interior particle board with shellac. This will seal in the waxes with which the board is made. On exterior panels, however, use a pigmented solvent-based primer.

For a final paint finish, apply a solvent-based alkyd (best) or latex. Shellac, varnish, or lacquer can be used for a clear finish. An application of stain can be made 24 hours before a clear finish is applied.

Pine Pine is the most common wood we use, one of the many reasons for this being that it takes and holds almost any kind of finish very well. The directions for painting wood apply as well to pine as to other woods. There are only a couple of special points to note:

Knots in pine very often bleed through any opaque finish applied over them. To prevent this when you are painting new pine, spot-prime the knots with WP-578 knot-sealer. If this is not available, use shellac or a pigmented stain-killer. On pine that has already been finished, cover the stains caused by bleeding knots with shellac or stain killer.

Before applying a natural finish to pine, be sure to test whatever stain you apply on a small piece of wood like that to be finished. There are many species of pine and they respond to a stain in various ways. The soft, white pines, for instance, soak up stain much more evenly than the hard, yellow pines. Whatever the species of pine boards you are staining, if you want the flattest, most even effect possible, brush thinned, boiled linseed oil over the surface just before applying an oil stain.

Plywood—fir and other construction woods Plywood made of Douglas fir and other softwoods, notably southern pine, is used extensively for interior and exterior work. Most of the panels are unfinished, but some made for exterior siding come with a factory-applied primer or even with a complete finish.

Because the grain of softwood plywood has a tendency to show through paint, all unfinished interior panels should be coated with a phenolic-resin primer-sealer after the initial sanding. When this has dried, sand again and dust well. Then apply an enamel undercoater tinted to the color of the final finish and follow with an alkyd enamel or wall paint.

If edges of plywood are exposed, as in a cabinet door, the pores should be filled by brushing on a couple of heavy coats of paste wood-filler. Fill large openings between the plies with spackle. An alternate way to make the edges smooth so they will not soak up a great deal of paint is to glue wood-veneer tapes over them.

Natural finishes on softwood plywood are not very attractive because the grain of the wood is wild and this is accentuated by the application of stain. Nevertheless, finishes of this kind are often used. To apply, simply sand the wood smooth and brush on an oil stain. Over this apply one or two coats of varnish or white shellac.

If you would prefer a natural finish, which subdues the plywood's contrasting grain pattern, brush on a phenolic-resin primer-sealer containing a white pigment; allow to stand for 15 minutes and wipe off most of it with a cloth. Sand when dry and apply a coat of thin, white shellac. Sand again and apply a thin coat of solvent-base enamel of any desired color. Wipe it off partially with a cloth. Sand once more. Then finish the job with a coat of flat varnish or white shellac.

Before the panels are installed, unfinished exterior plywood that is to be painted must have all edges sealed with a heavy coat of exterior oil-base primer or aluminum paint used on wood. Use the same finish on the face of the panels for a first coat. Then follow with two coats of any good house paint.

If exterior plywood is stained, apply two coats of exterior oil stain, either clear or opaque.

Plywood, hardwood Many decorative hardwood plywood panels are sold with a durable factory-applied clear finish; so your only worry about these is when they need refinishing. Wash thoroughly with detergent solution and go over every inch of surface with steel wool to remove any wax that may have been applied. Then apply one or two thin coats of white shellac. Varnish and lacquer can also be used.

Unfinished hardwood plywood is almost always given a natural finish because the wood is too beautiful to be covered with paint. First, go over the panels carefully with fine steel wool or fine sandpaper. Then, apply oil stain (if desired), and when this dries, work a paste wood-filler into the pores of open-grained woods. Sand again. Finish with a couple of coats of flat varnish if you need a very durable finish; otherwise, brush on a couple of coats of thinned white shellac.

Redwood This is a very attractive and durable wood that is used for many purposes both outside and inside the house. It can be finished in a variety of ways, depending on the location and the effect you want.

EXTERIOR REDWOOD This is often left unfinished. It gradually develops a mellow, silvery-gray color. However, in some climates, this transition may be temporarily interrupted by mildew, which turns the wood dark. To prevent this, it is a very good idea to apply a clear water-repellent containing pentachlorophenol. This retards the natural bleaching process and tends to produce a buckskin-tan color. Many repellents also contain a mildewcide.

The repellents are best applied by brush. The first coat should be followed by a second about six months later. Further treatment is unnecessary until the wood starts to darken (actually, in dry climates, this may never happen). Then apply one additional coat.

If you want redwood to turn a weathered, driftwood-gray color in a hurry, apply a bleaching oil. With the help of rain or periodic misting with a hose, a uniform color will be achieved in about six months. For an immediate effect, use a bleaching oil that contains a gray pigment.

Clear or pigmented oil-stains are used on redwood when a special color is desired. Oil-base and latex exterior paints may also be applied if, for some reason, you want to conceal the wood completely.

Two finishes that should never be used on exterior redwood are varnish and linseed oil.

INTERIOR REDWOOD   Redwood on ceilings and other areas out of reach of people and moisture is often left unfinished, but in areas where it will be exposed to dirt, abrasion, hand oils, moisture, and grease, you should always apply a clear penetrating-sealer. This gives good protection, retains the natural appearance of the wood, and needs little care.

Wax may also be used to retain the appearance of the wood, while protecting it to a limited degree, but it is not recommended because it is difficult to remove in case you should ever want to change to a different finish.

To change the color of interior redwood use a clear or, less desirable, pigmented oil-stain. To reduce soiling and improve cleanability this may be overcoated with white shellace and/or clear varnish.

Tileboard   This is a type of hardboard. The tile pattern is pressed into the panels, and a very durable factory finish is applied. This can, however, be covered with epoxy or alkyd enamel. The most important step is to wash the panels well and roughen the surface so the new enamel will hold.

how to paint masonry

This includes concrete, stucco, concrete blocks, cinder blocks, slag blocks, brick, stone, and tile. Asbestos-cement shingles are similar to masonry because they are made of cement, but they do not present the problems peculiar to masonry.

As a rule, masonry does not need paint to protect it, but it can be painted for decorative purposes, for waterproofing, or to make it easier to clean and maintain.

All forms of masonry, with the exception of dry stone walls, contain Portland cement, which in turn contains alkali. This is harmful to many types of paint. While the amount of alkali at the surface of the masonry will decrease with age and weathering, more may be brought to the surface if the interior of the masonry is damp. The best policy is to use alkali-resistant paints on any masonry surface, regardless of age and location.

There is a wide selection of alkali-resistant paints which give good results:

Latex is one of the best paints to apply to masonry inside and outside the house, but it is not suitable for cinder and slag blocks. Latex concrete floor enamels can be used on interior and exterior slabs. As there are many brands and types of latex paint, use only those specified for masonry.

Latex paints do best when applied to unpainted masonry that is slightly damp. If the surface has been previously painted and the old paint is chalking, a special primer is usually required before the latex goes on.

Solvent-thinned rubber-base paints, also known as chlorinated rubber paints, are highly resistant to alkali, water penetration, and abrasion. They are excellent for all concrete floors, except in garages, walls, swimming pools, walks, and terraces.

Use them on all cinder and slag blocks. Application is made to new as well as painted surfaces.

Catalytic coatings are epoxy finishes. They are particularly good where maximum adhesion and resistance to wear and moisture are of top importance. They must be applied directly to masonry and not over a previous coating.

Portland-cement paints come as dry powders, which are mixed with water and scrubbed into a damp masonry surface with a fiber brush. They cannot be used over old paint or other finish. When properly applied they become an integral part of the masonry and will not blister or peel.

Oil-base stucco and masonry paints are similar to ordinary house paints, except that they are reinforced with resins to make them more resistant to alkali. They are not suitable for new masonry or surfaces that become damp.

Concrete stains work in the same way as clear woodstains in that they are absorbed into the material and do not produce a surface coating.

Masonry sealers are colorless, penetrating materials that protect the masonry against stains and make it easier to clean.

A roller with a long nap is the most practical way to paint most masonry.

Brick, outdoors On new brick the best choice of paint is an exterior latex formulated for masonry. The first coat should be applied to a clean, damp surface. Two coats will usually be sufficient. Solvent-thinned rubber-base paints are also excellent, especially if it is necessary to improve a wall's resistance to water penetration.

A solvent-thinned rubber-base paint is also excellent—in fact, the top choice—on walls that have been previously painted. They adhere well to the old paint, even if it is chalking. Latex paints are also good but require a special primer to insure adhesion.

Before repainting a brick structure remove all loose or failing paint with a wire brush or, if necessary, paint remover. Scrub stains with detergent solution or a powdered household cleanser. Also remove moss and treat the bricks with poison (*see* moss). Apply the new paint with a long-napped roller.

Before painting brick, block, or stone, repair faulty mortar joints with mortar cement.

Portland-cement paints are also recommended for exterior brick but have lost favor in recent years because application is so tedious.

Brick, indoors   If brick is to be left natural but needs protection against soiling, clean it with a mild solution of muriatic acid to remove dirt and traces of mortar. Flush with clear water and allow to dry. Then brush on two coats of a transparent masonrysealer or a thinned white shellac.

If bricks are to be painted use latex interior wall-paint. On surfaces that are completely free of moisture a solvent-thinned wall paint may be used, too. In either case, two coats are usually required. Apply with a roller.

Bricks, glazed   These bricks have a smooth, dense, glazed surface similar to that on ceramic tile. They should be painted like ceramic tile.

Ceramic tile   The best kind of paint to use on tile is an epoxy. If the surface has been properly prepared and the paint applied in accordance with directions, it will produce a high-gloss finish that will be extremely durable and moisture resistant. Even surfaces that are exposed to streams of water will not peel.

Before applying the epoxy, wash the walls with detergent solution. Then go over them with a paste of powdered pumice and water to roughen the surface and remove the film left by the detergent. Pay particular attention to areas around lavatories, soap dishes, etc., which are likely to be coated with a soap film. Once the wall and fittings are clean and dry, the epoxy can be applied.

Alkyd wall enamel may also be used on ceramic tile but is less durable and cannot be expected to stand up for very long in damp areas.

Cinder blocks These are used in some sections of the country for basement walls, foundations, and exteriors. They differ from ordinary concrete blocks in that they are made of cement, sand and cinders, or slag, rather than cement, sand, and gravel. These ingredients often contain particles of iron that bleed through some kinds of paint. The acidity of the iron also may react on certain types of paint. Because of these problems, the best paint to apply to cinder block is a solvent-thinned rubber-base paint. Several coats are necessary to give good coverage of the rough surface. Apply with a spray gun or roller with a long nap.

Concrete Allow new concrete to dry thoroughly before it is painted. Concrete floors and swimming pools must be etched with muriatic acid, but this is generally not necessary on other concrete. If the concrete is dirty, scrub it with trisodium phosphate and rinse.

Old concrete should be scrubbed with the same cleaning compound. If oil and grease stains do not come up, treat them with one of the concrete floor cleaners used in service stations and often sold by them. Remove efflorescence with muriatic acid. Scrape off loose paint and other coatings. A disk sander does a quick job.

If concrete, new or old, is very porous, you can fill the voids (it isn't mandatory) with a grout made of Portland cement and water. The concrete should be sprinkled with water first; then brush the grout into the pores with a coarse-fiber brush and allow it to harden for several days. The alternative, which is more expensive but easier on a vertical surface, is to apply a block filler.

Apply two coats of latex masonry-paint, solvent-thinned rubber-base paint, or epoxy paint, depending on the finish desired, the location of the concrete, and how much work you are willing to do. *See* masonry. For a clear finish apply a masonry sealer that penetrates the pores and thus helps to prevent staining and improve cleaning. For a stain finish, *see* driveways. *Also see* floors, concrete; pools, concrete.

Concrete blocks These are painted in almost exactly the same way as concrete. The only differences are as follows:

Concrete blocks rarely need treatment with muriatic acid, unless they are very dirty or efflorescing. On the other hand, since concrete blocks are usually more porous than concrete, they are more likely to need pore filling. Use a prepared block filler.

The paints and masonry sealers recommended for concrete are equally good for concrete blocks. In addition, there is a special finish you should be familiar with in case you have a concrete-block basement wall that seeps water. This is a heavy-base cementitious coating made specifically for water-proofing masonry walls.

The coating comes as a powder, which is mixed with water to batter consistency. Several pastel colors are available.

Walls to be painted must be clean and free of efflorescence. If previously painted, most of the film must be removed. Active leaks must be plugged.

Wet the walls before painting. If the coating doesn't stick, apply more water. Brush the coating on with a fiber brush, work it into the blocks and don't try to spread it too far. For the first coat you should use about two pounds of powder per square yard. The second coat, applied 12 hours or more later, can be thinner. If leaking persists apply additional coats until you bring matters under control.

The ordinary brushed-on finish is quite rough. If you want a smooth finish, mix the powder with sand and water and apply it in a thick coat with a mason's trowel.

Like any other masonry surface, the cementitious coating can be overcoated when dry with latex masonry-paint or any other proper coating.

Flagstone See floors (flagstone and slate). When used outdoors flagstone is rarely coated with a masonry sealer. However, sealing might be advisable in areas that are unusually exposed to grease and stains.

Quarry tiles Quarry tiles are unglazed ceramic tiles that are generally laid on floors. They are best painted with epoxy floor enamel. Make sure they are clean and free of wax.

To maintain a clear, stainproof finish they may be treated with a masonry sealer.

Slag blocks Slag blocks are similar to cinder blocks.

Slate You can make slate more impervious to stains and easier to clean if you brush on a clear masonry-sealer every couple of years.

Stone To prevent staining and make for easier sweeping and washing of stone paving, benches, tables, and other horizontal surfaces, apply a clear masonry sealer every couple of years.

House garden walls made of stone may be painted with latex exterior-paint or Portland-cement paint. The former is better and easier to apply.

Remove any efflorescence on the walls with muriatic acid. Scrub the walls with a brush and hose them down under a hard stream to remove dirt. In cities, if the stone is very dirty, use a strong detergent solution; and in extreme cases, you will have to have the walls sand blasted.

The walls should be slightly damp when painted with latex. Use a spray gun or a roller with a long nap.

To mark boulders along the edges of driveways and roads, paint them with white latex.

Stucco Stucco is a somewhat porous concrete plaster. It need not be finished in any way, but it is a good idea to protect it with a silicone water-repellent or paint to prevent entrance of moisture.

New stucco should be allowed to set and dry thoroughly before it is painted. You can then brush, roll, or spray on two coats of an exterior latex paint made for masonry or a solvent-thinned rubber-base paint. Other paints mentioned under masonry may also be used, but do not offer any outstanding advantages.

Old painted stucco should be cleaned well—usually under a hose—to remove dirt. Patch deep holes and breaks with a mixture of 1 part Portland cement, 3 parts sand, and enough water to make a workable plastic. Wet the edges of the hole before troweling this in. The first patch should fill the hole only about to a third of its depth. After it has set, sprinkle it with water and keep it slightly damp for two days. Then apply a second patch to within about ¼ inch of the top surface and let it cure in the same way for two days. Then trowel in a prepared stucco mixture, which is available at masonry supply stores.

If holes and cracks are shallow or small use the prepared stucco mixture only.

Let the patches dry before applying paint.

how to paint metals

Metals found in and around the house are not difficult to paint. They may require more careful surface preparation than wood to insure a good bond between the paint and the metal. This is especially true of iron and steel because of the rust factor. But once the metal surface has been properly prepared and the correct primer and topcoats applied, it is usually possible to maintain a good painted surface with minimum upkeep, even on iron and steel that are exposed to the weather.

Aluminum This metal is found around the house in the form of exterior siding, windows and doors, screens and storm windows, gutters, indoor and outdoor furniture, sporting equipment, and so forth.

As a general rule, aluminum inside a building does not need painting, except for esthetic reasons. Cover it with any good grade of interior paint. Aluminum that is exposed to the weather, however, frequently develops a rough, powdery appearance unless protected with exterior paint or lacquer.

SURFACE PREPARATION After aluminum has been exposed to the atmosphere for a month or six weeks, a thin film of oxide forms on the surface. This may be almost invisible or it may be a quite obvious gray discoloration. The film tends to prevent further oxidation and also provides a very suitable base for paint. All that is necessary to prepare the surface is to wipe it clean of dirt. If the film is heavy, wipe with sandpaper or steel wool. The surface is then ready for priming.

New aluminum that has not been exposed to the atmosphere long enough for oxidation to occur requires special preparation to remove oil and grease resulting from the manufacturing process, as well as other coatings used to protect the metal during installation.

Wiping the surface with mineral spirits will usually remove most of the surface deposits, but it is best to use a metal conditioner containing phosphoric acid. Follow the directions on the label for the correct application of the conditioner.

PAINTING Aluminum can be primed with any wood or metal primer or one made especially for aluminum. If the atmosphere has a high concentration of industrial fumes, it is best to use a primer containing zinc chromate. In any event, it is essential that a good quality primer be applied.

Use two finish coats over the primer. Select the proper paint for the location of the aluminum—exterior paints for aluminum exposed to the weather; interior paints for aluminum indoors. Latex, oil, or alkyd paints are all satisfactory.

REPAINTING Many aluminum products, such as siding and roofing, come with a factory-applied finish that will last for many years. If a change of color is desired or if the finish becomes faded, applying a fresh coat of paint is an easy matter.

A surface in good condition should be rubbed lightly with steel wool or sandpaper to cut the gloss of the old paint and thus insure good adhesion of the new. If there are spots where the finish has chipped or peeled, remove the loose paint and sand the edges to a feather-edge. Coat the exposed metal with a primer and then apply new paint to the entire surface.

NATURAL FINISH If you wish to retain the natural color of aluminum and to prevent oxidation, coat with a clear lacquer. If the metal is still new and bright, wipe with a solvent and rub with fine steel wool. If it has become discolored, treat with a metal conditioner containing phosphoric acid, and rub with steel wool until the metal is bright. Then apply one or two coats of a clear, non-yellowing acrylic or cellulose-butyrate lacquer.

Brass For a clear finish remove old lacquer (if any) with lacquer thinner. Clean metal with fine steel wool and household ammonia (as it comes from the bottle) and rinse well. Then spray or brush on clear lacquer.

If you paint brass, do not remove the tarnish because it helps to hold the paint. Wash off dirt and grease with a detergent solution. Prime with a metal primer and finish with a zinc-free enamel.

Bronze Handle like brass.

Chrome Chrome that is slightly scratched can be improved by applying a chrome cleaner and protector, which is available at auto-supply stores. If the chrome has been chipped or scraped from the steel base, remove rust and brush on a metal primer. Then apply a chrome-finish aluminum paint.

To paint over chrome you must first roughen the finish with emery cloth to give the primer, which follows, something to grip to. Overcoat the primer with enamel made for metal.

Copper If you want a clear finish, clean the copper with fine steel wool and household ammonia straight from the bottle. Rinse well. Spray or brush with a clear lacquer.

To preserve the color, or patina, of old weathered copper, simply clean with a detergent solution and spray with clear lacquer. Outside the house use spar varnish.

To paint copper, do not remove the tarnish but clean the metal well. Go over the green areas with steel wool to remove as much of the oxide as possible. Then apply any good metal primer, followed by one or two coats of metal enamel, exterior trim enamel, or interior alkyd-paint.

Galvanized steel Often called galvanized iron, this is steel to which a coating of zinc has been applied to make it corrosion resistant. Galvanized steel is found around the house in the form of gutters and downspouts, flashing, garbage cans, mail boxes, and sometimes roofing material. It is used extensively on farms for roofing and siding.

As long as the zinc coating remains intact, galvanized steel will not corrode and therefore does not require painting. However, it may be painted for the sake of appearance, for greater heat reflection, or to extend its life. After some years of exposure to the weather, the zinc coating will wear away and then corrosion of the steel will start.

Most galvanized steel contains an inhibitor that interferes with adhesion of paint until the inhibitor is removed. The easiest way to accomplish this is simply to expose the steel to the weather for about six months. The steel is then ready for painting.

It is essential to prime galvanized steel with a primer designed for the metal. Among the best are those containing approximately 80 percent zinc dust and 20 percent zinc oxide in an oil vehicle; but other equally good primers are on the market. Stir the primer frequently to keep the zinc in suspension: it is a heavy pigment and tends to settle. When painting old galvanized steel that has weathered for many years, rust spots that have appeared must be removed with sandpaper before the primer is applied.

Because some paints are not compatible with certain primers, be sure to use a paint made or recommended by the maker of the primer for the topcoats. Or use a primer recommended by the manufacturer of the topcoat. In either case, two topcoats should be applied.

Iron and steel   Any object made of these materials that is exposed to the weather or is in a damp location, such as the basement, must be coated with a rust-inhibiting primer, followed by two or more topcoats of paint.

NEW WORK   Wipe it clean with a solvent, such as mineral spirits, to remove the thin coating of oil or grease usually applied at the factory to prevent rusting during transportation and installation. Unless this coating is removed, paint will not adhere to the metal. If there are any traces of rust, remove these with sandpaper; then coat the metal with a rust-inhibiting metal primer, followed by two or more coats of exterior metal-enamel.

OLD WORK   If the old paint film is in good condition and there are no areas where it has cracked, chipped off, or rusted, wipe down the paint with sandpaper or steel wool to cut the gloss. Clean the surface with mineral spirits or turpentine and then apply fresh paint. If the old paint is in poor condition, it should be removed. The best way to do this is with a paint remover.

If rust has appeared it should be removed. While you can prevent rust from forming if you cover the metal with a primer and several coats of paint, if you apply paint over metal that is already rusted, there is no certainty that the rust will not continue to grow. Some of the newer metal-primers claim that they can be used over rust, but it is better to play it safe and remove all traces of rust.

The usual way of doing this is to go over the rusted area with some kind of scraper or coarse file. If the rust is very thick, chip it off with a cold chisel. Then rub the area vigorously with a wire brush, steel wool, emery cloth, or sandpaper.

A stiff wire-brush is effective in removing loose rust from iron and steel.

It is a good idea to follow this treatment by coating the metal with a metal conditioner containing phosphoric acid. This gets into crevices and holes you cannot reach by sanding, and it conditions the metal to allow the primer to make a good bond. After this, apply a rust-inhibiting primer, followed by two or more coats of paint.

Preventing rust from forming is, of course, just as important as removing it, and in the long run, it will save you a lot of work. There are three simple rules to follow:

1. Don't leave bare iron and steel exposed too long. This is particularly important outdoors, but don't assume that metal indoors will not rust if water gets on it or the atmosphere is damp. Apply a primer as soon as possible.

2. Don't clean bare iron and steel with water. Use a solvent, such as mineral spirits, benzine, or naphtha.

3. Don't apply a water-based paint to bare iron and steel because it will cause immediate rusting. The exception is the latex metal-primers especially designed for application to bare metal.

Lead   Wash with detergent solution and rub lightly with fine steel wool to remove roughness. Then brush on a solvent-based primer used on exterior trim. Follow with a solvent-based trim paint.

Pewter   Pewter is finished only to prevent tarnishing. First clean the metal with household ammonia and fine steel wool. Rinse and dry. Then spray on a couple of coats of clear lacquer.

Stainless steel   Wash to remove grease. Roughen the surface with emery cloth. Apply an epoxy primer and epoxy enamel, or a metal primer and metal enamel.

Tin   In Colonial days, painted tinware was produced by

thousands of families and little businesses. With modern paints, you can produce even more durable finishes, though they won't necessarily be any prettier.

Rub tin with fine steel wool to subdue the shine. Then apply a solvent-base primer and compatible enamel. Epoxy will prove most durable, although alkyd is excellent, too. Spray enamels are especially easy to work with if you give tin an overall background color.

Wrought iron Wrought iron is much more resistant to corrosion than iron or steel but should be treated in the same way

how to paint the outside of a house

Houses that are painted usually need to be repainted every four or five years. More frequent painting is rarely recommended because it does not give the old paint-film enough time to wear away (a paint that is too thick is brittle and does not provide a good bond for the new paint). Less frequent painting is permissible as long as the old paint film looks decent and provides the protection required.

Houses that are covered with a pigmented stain often do not require refinishing as often as painted houses; but don't count on it. On the other hand, if your house has been given a natural finish, you can be reasonably sure it will have to be refinished every two or three years, because such finishes are rapidly destroyed by the sun.

Whatever your painting schedule, the work should be done in dry weather when the temperature ranges between 50 and 80 degrees. There should be little wind, especially if the surrounding ground is bare dirt, and few insects. In most parts of the country, fall is usually the ideal time for house painting.

HOUSE PAINTS These are the paints that are used on outside walls of houses and other buildings.

LINSEED-OIL PAINTS These are solvent-thinned paints, which are most commonly referred to as "house paints." They cover well and have good ability to adhere to many different surfaces and surface conditions. They can be applied directly to previously painted surfaces that are chalking. They can also be applied directly to surfaces on which old paint is badly worn. On the other hand, oil paints are not as suitable for new masonry as latex paints because they can be damaged by alkalis in the

An old or inexpensive brush is excellent for dusting surfaces before painting.

masonry; but they can be used on masonry with an old paint film that is still sound.

Some oil paints are so-called "chalking paints," meaning that as they weather the surface gradually wears away. Thus the paints are self-cleaning Other paints are formulated to be chalk resistant. There are also mildew- and fume-resistant oil paints.

Compared with latex house-paints, linseed-oil paints are slow lrying. This can be a disadvantage on windy and buggy days; but it can also be an advantage on hot, dry days when a water base paint may dry too rapidly.

LINSEED-OIL EMULSION PAINTS These combine many of the advantages of a linseed-oil paint with those of water emulsion paints. The paints adhere well to old paint and can be applied to damp surfaces.

LATEX EXTERIOR PAINTS These have become most popular with home owners because of their ease of application and clean-up, fast drying, etc. They are good for both wood and masonry, but require a special primer for application to bare wood and over old paint that is chalking.

ONE-COAT HOUSE PAINTS These heavily pigmented oil or latex paints are designed for use over previously primed or painted surfaces that are in good condition. They should never be applied to bare wood; and they should not be applied too thickly because they will not adhere properly.

The main advantage of one-coat house paint is that you don't have to apply a second coat. They give excellent coverage, though it is no better, and often not as good, as the coverage you get with two coats of ordinary house paint. On the other hand, the one-coat paints are the most expensive available, and they are not the easiest to apply.

In industrial areas and wherever the atmosphere is badly polluted use a fume-resistant exterior paint. Be sure that the paint you use contains a mildewcide if you live in a humid climate or a damp, shady pocket.

PIGMENTED OIL-STAINS These are recommended for wood and plywood siding because they color the wood and protect it but don't completely conceal the grain. They are especially desirable on shingles, shakes, and other rough-textured lumber because they penetrate deeply and generally outlast paint.

CLEAR FINISHES In many areas, particularly near the seacoast, the best clear finish is none at all. Wood can be allowed to weather naturally and beautifully; or you can hasten the process, without affecting the ultimate beauty, by brushing on a bleaching oil.

If you want to retain the color of new wood, apply two coats of a water repellent formulated for wood. Additional treatment becomes necessary only when the wood begins to darken.

If you want to change the natural color of the wood, apply a clear oil-stain and overcoat it with a clear penetrating wood-sealer. If you want to maintain the natural color of the wood, just apply a wood sealer. No other clear finish should be used on siding, because it will break down rapidly under the ultra-violet rays of the sun. (The wood sealers break down, too, but not so rapidly.)

Use a colorless silicone water-repellent on masonry siding if you want to keep out moisture without changing the appearance of the siding.

TRIM PAINTS On houses that are painted or covered with a pigmented stain, an alkyd trim and shutter enamel is the best for all the trim, doors, and windows. Spar varnish is generally used if a natural finish is the aim; but because of its poor resistance to the sun, it should really be limited to doors, which need a hard finish to protect them against soiling, scuffing, and hand oils. If your decorating scheme permits you to use a penetrating wood-sealer on other trim, use it.

PREPARATION Remove shutters and screens. Even if the for-

	HOUSE PAINT	TRANSPARENT SEALER (OIL)	CEMENT BASE PAINT	EXTERIOR CLEAR FINISH	ALUMINUM PAINT	WOOD STAIN	ROOF COATING	ASPHALT EMULSION	ROOF CEMENT	TRIM AND TRELLIS PAINT	AWNING PAINT	SPAR VARNISH	PORCH AND DECK PAINT	PRIMER OR UNDERCOATER	METAL PRIMER	LATEX TYPES	WATER REPELLANT PRESERVATIVES
CLAPBOARD SIDING	●			✓										✓		✓	
BRICK	●	✓	✓	✓										✓		✓	
CEMENT & CINDER BLOCK	●	✓	✓	✓										✓		✓	
ASBESTOS CEMENT	●													✓		✓	
STUCCO	●	✓	✓	✓										✓		✓	
NATURAL WOOD SIDING & TRIM				✓		✓						✓					
METAL SIDING	●			●						●					✓	●	
WOOD FRAME WINDOWS	●			✓						●				✓		●	
STEEL WINDOWS	●			●						●					✓	●	
ALUMINUM WINDOWS	●			✓						●					✓	●	
SHUTTERS & OTHER TRIM	●									●				✓		●	
CANVAS AWNINGS											✓						
WOOD SHINGLE ROOF						✓											✓
METAL ROOF	●														✓	●	
COAL TAR FELT ROOF							✓	✓	✓								
WOOD PORCH FLOOR													✓				
CEMENT PORCH FLOOR													✓		✓		
COPPER SURFACES													✓				
GALVANIZED SURFACES	●			●						●				✓	✓	●	
IRON SURFACES	●			●						●					✓	●	

● Black dot indicates that a primer or sealer may be necessary before the finishing coat (unless surface has been previously finished.)

Exterior paints and finishes, which one to use, and where.

mer are screwed to the house, it is advisable to take them down so you can inspect, clean, and paint the wall behind them.

Remove downspouts for much the same reason.

Clean all surfaces thoroughly. As a rule, the trim—especially window sills and other horizontal surfaces—needs most careful attention. But when you inspect the walls closely, you will be amazed at the amount of dirt, mildew, cobwebs, and so forth, you will find on them. Often a hard scrubbing with a dry-bristle brush will take care of matters; but don't be reluctant to get out a bucket of detergent solution and/or a garden hose. Thorough washing is commonly needed in built-up areas—especially industrial areas—and for very rough brick and stone surfaces.

Any house within 25 miles of the coast should be washed with fresh water before painting to remove salt deposits that would interfere with the proper drying of the new finish. Apply paint immediately. If you wait even for a day or so, salt deposits will again build up and you must wash the house again.

Remove rust stains and copper stains with a strong solution of trisodium phosphate.

When all surfaces are clean, go over them for defects in the old finish. If you find blisters, you may have a moisture condition in the walls that must be corrected before a new finish is applied (see paint, problems and failures). Scrape off blisters, peeling and loose paint. Sand rough edges and areas. In very bad situations, strip the paint down to the base material with heat or a chemical paint-remover.

Repair cracks, holes, and breaks in the siding and trim. Repair and rehang gutters that overflow and stain or soil the walls.

Blistered and peeling paint should be removed with a putty knife.

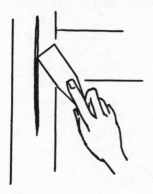

Use putty or exterior spackling compound to fill cracks and holes in outside woodwork before painting.

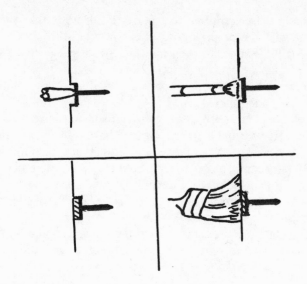

Use a nail set to drive nail heads below wood surface. Dab
paint on nail head. Fill in over nail head with putty and then
spot-prime the putty.

Reglaze windows as necessary. Counter-sink protruding nails,
cover them with putty, and then spot-prime. Spot-prime stains
caused by knots bleeding through.

Pull shrubs and trees that rub against the house away, or tie
them up mummy-fashion. Take down vines if you expect to
paint the walls behind them. When you are actually painting,
toss drop cloths over all plants growing close to the house.

If you use anything other than a water-base paint, make sure
the walls are thoroughly dry.

APPLYING THE PAINT   If the old finish on the house is in poor
condition, or if you are painting a house that has never been
painted before, apply the appropriate primer as the first coat.
But no primer is needed over a sound finish. In either case, one
finish coat generally gives more than adequate coverage.

Apply paint, stain, or clear finish with a brush or roller, which-
ever seems easier. On flat surfaces, such as brick, concrete block,
and plywood, a roller is preferred. On irregular surfaces, such as
shingles, clapboards, and stone, a brush is usually better, because

Bare wood must be spot-primed even when one-coat house paint is used.

it enables you to work paint into cracks, joints, pores, and other hard-to-paint places.

Work in the shade as much as possible. For one thing, it is more comfortable and easier on the eyes. More important, you can see places you missed better than when you are blinded by the sun's glare. In addition, the finish dries at its normal pace.

Paint the eaves, rakes, and cornices first. Then, starting at one upper corner, paint the siding across the house in a deep band to the next corner or to an intervening door or window. Then drop down and paint another band across the house. Continue in this way until the siding on that side of the house is finished. If you can't do the entire side of a house in one day, stop work at the edge of a door or window. This reduces lap marks.

When the siding is completed, paint the trim, windows, doors, gutters, and so forth. Finish with the shutters and screens.

NEW HOUSES Painting a new house isn't very different from painting an old one except that there is no question about the need for at least two coats of all finishes. Except for finishes that serve as their own primer, start with a primer and complete the job with a compatible finish-coat. To avoid intercoat peeling, the finish coat should be put on within two weeks after the first coat.

Unless you are giving wood or plywood a clear finish, there is no need to hurry to get your house painted or stained. Several month's weathering will not hurt, and it gives unseasoned wood a chance to dissipate some of its moisture. It is also a good idea to allow masonry walls to go unfinished for a while in order to give them a chance to dry out.

If the roof of your house is	You can paint the body	Pink	Bright red	Red-orange	Tile red	Cream	Bright yellow	Light green	Dark green	Gray-green	Blue-green	Light blue	Dark blue	Blue-gray	Violet	Brown	White
GRAY	White	X	X	X	X	X	X	X	X	X	X	X	X	X	X		
	Gray	X	X	X	X			X	X	X	X	X	X	X	X		X
	Cream-yellow		X		X		X		X	X							X
	Pale green				X		X		X	X							X
	Dark green	X				X	X	X									X
	Putty			X	X				X	X			X	X		X	
	Dull red	X				X		X						X			X
GREEN	White	X	X	X	X	X	X	X	X	X	X	X	X	X	X	X	
	Gray			X			X	X	X								X
	Cream-yellow		X		X			X	X	X						X	X
	Pale green			X	X		X		X								X
	Dark green	X		X		X	X	X									X
	Beige			X					X	X		X	X				
	Brown	X				X	X	X									X
	Dull red				X		X		X								X
RED	White		X		X				X		X			X			
	Light gray		X		X				X								X
	Cream-yellow		X		X						X		X	X			
	Pale green		X		X												X
	Dull red					X		X		X	X						X
BROWN	White			X	X			X	X	X	X		X	X	X	X	
	Buff				X				X	X	X				X		
	Pink-beige				X				X	X					X	X	
	Cream-yellow				X				X	X	X				X		
	Pale green				X				X	X					X		
	Brown		X			X	X										X
BLUE	White		X	X		X						X	X				
	Gray		X		X							X	X				X
	Cream-yellow		X	X									X	X			
	Blue		X		X	X						X					X

Suggested color schemes for the exterior of house. If the house has shutters, paint the trim the same color as the body of house or white. If not, use these suggested colors for trim.

Asbestos-cement shingles and boards These materials are made of asbestos fibers and Portland cement. Because the cement contains alkalies, which can be harmful to many standard oil-base paints, the best finish to use is a latex exterior paint. Solvent-thinned resin paints may be used, too.

Before painting, remove dust and other foreign matter with a wire brush. Wash off imbedded dirt with a strong detergent solution. Latex paints can be applied over the shingles and boards while they are still damp. Use either brush or roller. Two coats are usually required.

Solvent-thinned resin paints must be applied to an absolutely dry surface. With some brands, a special primer is required. In other cases, the same paint is used for both primer and finish.

Gutters These may be of aluminum, copper, galvanized steel, vinyl, or wood. Some types of gutters are built into the cornice, but most are hung from the eaves or cornice on straps or brackets. Gutters and downspouts are usually painted along with the exterior of the house.

Before painting gutters, check to make sure they are functioning properly. They must have a slight pitch so that water dripping into them will drain to the downspouts. If they are not properly pitched, water will collect at one point and overflow the sides, causing staining of the adjacent surfaces and possibly causing the exterior paint to blister and peel. Low spots will also develop in gutters that are not properly supported. Put water in each gutter with a garden hose to check the flow; and adjust or add straps or brackets to change the pitch.

Downspouts are sometimes clogged by an accumulation of leaves and other debris. The downspout opening should be protected with a strainer of some type. Check the flow of water through the downspout with a garden hose. Joints between the downspout and gutter should be tight to prevent leakage.

Tree leaves are the great enemy of all gutters. If they are allowed to accumulate, they will hasten the corrosion or decay of the gutters. The weight of an accumulation of wet leaves may also pull gutters loose or cause them to sag and overflow. If you have deciduous trees near the house, it is wise to cover the gutters with ¼-inch wire mesh or prefabricated gutter guards.

ALUMINUM GUTTERS These often come with a factory finish

that will last a good many years. If a change of color is desired, clean the surface, rub with medium sandpaper, and apply the same paint used on the exterior trim.

Aluminum gutters without a factory finish do not as a rule require painting except for appearance. If they are to be painted, use the same color as the cornice or siding. The painting procedure is described under aluminum.

COPPER GUTTERS These are generally left unfinished and allowed to turn an attractive brown or green. When this happens, however, water dripping from green portions of the metal may stain the adjacent walls. It is a good idea, therefore, to paint copper gutters with exterior trim enamel or spar varnish.

GALVANIZED STEEL GUTTERS These will rust out in short order if not painted. Follow directions under galvanized steel for finishing the exterior surfaces. To prevent rusting of the gutters on the inside, clean out the troughs, wire-brush away all loose rust and apply an asphalt roofing cement. A rather thick coating will provide good protection for several years.

VINYL GUTTERS These do not require a protective coating but can be painted according to directions (*see* vinyl, rigid).

WOOD GUTTERS Wood gutters should be thoroughly impregnated with a paintable wood-preservative before they are hung. Thereafter, you should keep the troughs coated with asphalt roofing-cement or special gutter paints. Paint exterior surfaces with alkyd trim enamel.

Downspouts The best way to paint downspouts, or leaders, is to take them down off the house. This will enable you to examine them more carefully for leaks, to make necessary repairs, and to sand the old finish smooth. You can also paint the back of the spouts without streaking up the house wall. And you can, at the same time, paint or stain the house wall behind the spouts.

For how to paint aluminum downspouts, *see* aluminum; for galvanized steel downspouts, *see* galvanized steel. Copper downspouts should be wiped clean and rubbed with steel wool as necessary to take off products of corrosion. Then brush on exterior trim enamel or spar varnish. Vinyl downspouts are usually not painted. *See also* gutters.

Flashing Although the metal flashing on buildings is generally left unfinished, there are times when painting is advisable.

Copper flashing may be painted if water dripping off the green oxide, which forms on the metal, stains wall surfaces below. Before painting, remove as much of the oxide as possible with steel wool and household ammonia or metal polish. Then brush on any type of solvent-base exterior house-paint.

Aluminum flashing may be painted simply to conceal its shiny surface. If the aluminum has weathered for six weeks or more, you can paint right over it with a solvent-base house paint; but if it has not weathered, it should first be etched and cleaned with a metal conditioner.

Galvanized-steel flashing should always be painted to prevent rusting. Use asphalt roofing-cement.

Porches If a porch is built of wood it is best painted like a deck (*see* decks, wood). Porch and deck enamel may, of course, be used on the floor, but it doesn't wear very well because the floor is usually exposed on the underside to damp soil and, consequently, is quite damp itself.

For maximum durability and ease of cleaning, concrete porch floors are best painted with an epoxy primer and enamel formulated for use on paving.

Porch railings, columns, and so forth are finished with alkyd trim enamel. If a railing has numerous small balusters, try painting them with a painter's mitt.

Roofs Roofs covered with asphalt shingles, asphalt roll-roofing, built-up tar and gravel, or metal can be painted with special roof paints. But wood shingles should never be painted, since that will encourage decay. They may, however, be stained.

The primary reason for painting a roof is to lengthen its life; but a roof that has deteriorated badly and begun to leak is beyond hope. Painting is also done to improve the appearance of a roof. And paints containing aluminum flakes are used to lower indoor temperatures by reflecting the sun's heat away from the roof.

As far as appearance goes, roof coatings are no substitute for a new roof and are therefore seldom used on the main house roof except for reasons of economy. They are, however, often used on outbuildings and for roofs over porches, bow windows, and similar small areas.

Roof coatings are available in black, aluminum, and a variety of colors. There are four types:

Asphalt fibered roof-coatings are black or aluminum liquids suitable for application by brush, roller, or spray gun. The type containing aluminum flakes is more resistant to wear.

Asphalt non-fibered roof-coatings are used primarily as a primer over dried-out roofing. The type containing aluminum, however, can be used as a finish coat. Apply by brush or spray.

Asphalt emulsion roof-coatings contain fine bituminous particles suspended in water. Application is by brush or spray.

Colored aluminum roof-coatings contain aluminum flakes and come in various colors. They can be applied by brush or spray.

SURFACE PREPARATION The roof should be clean and free of dirt, dust, and loose rust. Remove loose gravel and mineral particles. Replace torn or missing shingles. Patch holes, cracks, and broken seams with asphalt roofing-cement and allow the patch to dry thoroughly before applying the roof coating.

Roofs should be dry before coating. However, asphalt-emulsion coatings can be applied to a damp surface provided there is no chance of rain for the following 24 hours.

Start painting at the highest point of the roof and work down. If the work is done by brush and the surface is large, use a special long-handled roof brush.

WOOD SHINGLES Use an exterior oil-stain similar to that used on siding. Shingles are best stained before application to the roof, but you can do the job easily enough afterwards with a roller, brush, or spray gun.

Shutters Use a shutter and trim enamel on shutters (the same kind as is used for other exterior trim). Solid shutters can be easily painted with a brush. Louvered shutters are best done with a spray gun. It is a lot easier to paint any shutter if it is taken down and tilted back against a wall. However, many shutters today are not hung on hinges but screwed directly to the window trim and siding. Although these are a nuisance to take down and put up again, it is a good idea to do so, because you can more easily paint the edges of the shutters, and you can also inspect the condition of the paint and siding behind them.

All shutters, but especially those on the street side of the house, pick up a good deal of dirt and should be thoroughly cleaned before painting. Use a household-detergent solution and rinse the shutters with a garden hose. Give them plenty of time to dry.

Most shutters are made of wood, but more and more aluminum and plastic units are being installed. These do not present any great problem in repainting. Wood shutters, however, should be inspected for holes and cracks.

If the shutters have movable louvers and you wish them to remain movable, apply a very thin coat of paint to the area where the louvers fit into the vertical rails. If the paint is too thick, the louvers can't be moved. Just as soon as the paint is dry enough to touch, it is wise to move the louvers in order to break any paint seal that may have formed.

Storm windows COMBINATIONS As these are made of aluminum, they require paint only for decorative purposes. Use an alkyd exterior trim enamel.

The best way to paint combination storm windows is to lift out the storm panels and screen panel. These can be painted individually and then replaced in the frame after they are dry. Use a wire brush to remove dirt from the metal.

CONVENTIONAL STORM WINDOWS These are one-piece windows that are put up in the fall and taken down in the spring. They have either wood or aluminum frames. When painting wood windows, replace faulty putty around the glass. Wash all surfaces and sand as necessary. Then apply an alkyd exterior trim enamel.

Aluminum frames may be unfinished or covered with factory-applied baked enamel. Generally these do not require painting, but if they do, follow directions under aluminum (which *see*).

Insulating siding This is a rigid insulation-board composed of vegetable fibers that are partially impregnated with asphalt. The exposed, or weather, side is coated with mineral granules and is often embossed and textured to resemble shingles, brick, stone, or clapboards.

Insulating siding does not normally require paint for protection, but it may be painted for decorative purposes. To prevent the asphalt from bleeding through the paint, use only a water-thinned paint that contains no solvents. Special paints designed for use on the siding are sold, but if you cannot lay hands on one, use an exterior latex-paint designed for masonry.

If stains do not soon appear in a coat of water-thinned paint, the asphalt is probably sealed in. In this event, an exterior house-paint that contains solvents can be applied over the latex. But you may, of course, continue with the latex alone.

The siding does not have to be dry for painting with latex, but it should be clean. Dust with a stiff brush. Use a strong detergent solution to wash off grease and other grime. The prime coat should be applied liberally to produce a coat thick enough to give a continuous film and, especially, to cover the granules. Since the surface is relatively rough, a gallon of paint will probably not cover more than 150 to 180 square feet. Apply the paint with brush, roller, or spray gun.

Decks, canvas Because decks are normally subject to wear and must be watertight, they should be kept coated with paint at all times. The best types of paint to use are alkyd porch and deck enamel or a marine deck paint. Both can be applied with brush or roller.

For how to apply, *see* boats (canvas decks and cabin tops).

Decks, wood Paints are not recommended for wood decks. The most satisfactory finish is a pigmented exterior oil-stain. A stain is easier to apply than paint, requires minimum surface preparation, and can be renewed easily. It does not hide the texture of the wood and will not peel or blister.

Stains should be applied to a new deck as soon as possible after the deck is built. If the raw wood is allowed to weather too long it will develop an uneven appearance, and the grain may begin to check.

Several types of stain are available for use on decks. Heavy-bodied stains contain a considerable amount of pigment and produce a durable, opaque coating that conceals the wood grain and color but not the texture. Semi-transparent stains contain less pigment and usually will not conceal the grain. Decking stains are especially designed for all walking surfaces, such as decks, steps, and ramps. Bleaching stains containing a weathering agent are designed for new wood. After several months' exposure, the wood will turn a silvery-gray.

Wood should be dry before application of a stain. Use a brush or spray gun. Apply the stain liberally but as evenly as possible. The underside as well as the edges of the deck should be coated. Ideally the first coat of stain should be applied to the planks before they are nailed in place; then you can be sure that the edges will be well covered.

If a deck has previously been painted, stain cannot be applied unless the paint is removed or has been so worn that the grain shows clearly. The most logical approach is to repaint the deck with an exterior deck enamel.

Basement bulkheads Finish new steel bulkheads, which come with a prime coat, with two coats of alkyd exterior-trim paint. Later, when rust spots begin to appear, sand them promptly and apply a liquid or jellied rust remover. Then prime with red lead and touch up with finish paint.

Wood bulkheads should be thoroughly treated with a paintable pentachlorophenol wood-preservative before they are painted. Then apply an alkyd primer and two coats of alkyd trim paint. Inspect the doors and bulkhead walls regularly thereafter; scrape off peeling paint and touch up with new finish.

The finish on all bulkheads and the bulkheads themselves deteriorate rapidly because they are exposed to rain and snow on the outside and to a certain amount of leakage and condensation inside. Rather constant and unrewarding attention is therefore essential. But you should avoid repainting them completely every time they are in need of help, because you would soon build up an extremely thick, brittle paint film that would actually give less protection to the steel or wood than a much thinner film.

Awnings, aluminum If the aluminum has not been previously painted, rub with steel wool to remove surface deposits. New awnings that have not been exposed to the weather should be treated with a metal conditioner and primed with wood or metal primer. Finish with two coats of exterior trim enamel.

Awnings that have been previously painted should be washed with a detergent solution to remove dirt and rubbed with steel wool to cut the gloss of the finish. Apply one or two coats of trim enamel. *See* aluminum.

Awnings, canvas Awnings that have not been treated with a waterproofing compound can be painted with a special canvas paint. Hold the canvas up to the light and if you can see through the weave, the fabric will take paint. Clean the awnings before painting. Wash with a detergent solution if they are badly soiled and allow them to dry thoroughly. Then brush or sprav on the paint.

Garage doors Finish garage doors made of wood, hardboard, steel, or aluminum with a solvent-base exterior trim enamel. In preparing the surface, pay particular attention to the bottom 18 inches because snow piles up against this area and rain bounces up on it from the apron. Look for rotting wood, open joints, rust.

Fiberglass doors do not need painting, but if you want to change the color, roughen the surface well with sandpaper and apply an epoxy primer and enamel.

Log cabins These are usually allowed to weather naturally, but there is no reason why you shouldn't apply a color of your choice.

Remove the bark first. New logs should be allowed to season for several months. If it is advisable to protect the logs against rot and termites, apply a creosote stain. Otherwise, you can use any clear or pigmented exterior oil stain. Brush on two coats.

Walls, exterior See asphalt-cement shingles and boards; brick; cedar; concrete; hardboard; insulating siding; masonry; plywood—fire and other construction woods; redwood; trim; vinyl, rigid; wood.

how to paint the
inside of a house

Because a non-reflecting paint is more restful to look at than one with a shine, walls and ceilings in most rooms of the house are usually coated with a latex or alkyd flat paint. In kitchens and bathrooms, however, semi-gloss or gloss alkyds are used because they are water-resistant and easier to clean. Use a semi-gloss or gloss alkyd or latex enamel on all woodwork.

LIGHT REFLECTANCES When selecting colors for the walls and ceilings of a room, consider the light reflectances of the various colors. Dark colors absorb light; light colors reflect it. If a room does not get much light naturally, select colors to make it lighter. If it gets too much natural light, dark colors may be indicated.

The reflectance values of several different colors follow:

White	80 percent	Apple-green	51 percent
Ivory (light)	71 percent	Gray (medium)	43 percent
Apricot-beige	66 percent	Green (light)	41 percent
Lemon-yellow	65 percent	Blue (pale)	41 percent
Ivory	59 percent	Rose (deep)	12 percent
Peach	53 percent	Green (dark)	9 percent
Salmon	53 percent		

When refinishing a room, paint the ceiling first, then walls, then woodwork. Baseboards should be painted after all other trim has been done. If floors are to be painted or refinished, they should be done last of all.

OLD WORK Get as much light furniture and so forth out of the room as possible. Group remaining pieces that are too heavy to move into the middle of the room and cover them with drop

	FLAT PAINT	SEMI-GLOSS PAINT	ENAMEL	CASEIN	INTERIOR VARNISH	SHELLAC	WAX (LIQUID OR PASTE)	WAX (EMULSION)	STAIN	WOOD SEALER	FLOOR SEALER	FLOOR VARNISH	ALUMINUM PAINT	SEALER OR UNDERCOATER	METAL PRIMER	LATEX TYPES
PLASTER WALLS & CEILING	✓•	✓•		✓										✓		✓
WALL BOARD	✓•	✓•		✓										✓		✓
WOOD PANELING	✓•	✓•			✓	✓	✓		✓	✓						✓•
KITCHEN & BATHROOM WALLS		✓•	✓•											✓		
WOOD FLOORS						✓	✓	✓•	✓•	✓	✓•	✓				
CONCRETE FLOORS							✓•	✓•	✓			✓				✓
VINYL & RUBBER TILE FLOORS							✓	✓								
ASPHALT TILE FLOORS								✓								
LINOLEUM							✓	✓	✓		✓	✓				
STAIR TREADS								✓		✓	✓	✓	✓			
STAIR RISERS	✓•	✓•			✓	✓			✓	✓						
WOOD TRIM	✓•	✓•			✓	✓	✓		✓					✓		✓•
STEEL WINDOWS	✓•	✓•											✓		✓	✓•
ALUMINUM WINDOWS	✓•	✓•											✓		✓	✓•
WINDOW SILLS					✓											
STEEL CABINETS	✓•	✓•												✓		
HEATING DUCTS	✓•	✓•											✓		✓	✓•
RADIATORS & HEATING PIPES	✓•	✓•											✓		✓	✓•
OLD MASONRY	✓	✓		✓									✓	✓		✓
NEW MASONRY	✓•	✓•												✓		✓

✓• Black dot indicates that a primer or sealer may be necessary before the finishing coat (unless surface has been previously finished.)

Interior paints and finishes, which one to use, and where.

cloths. Fill holes and cracks with spackle or patching plaster. Sand down rough seams between sections of gypsum board. If only one finish coat is to be applied, prime all patches with the same paint that will be used for the final coat.

Remove door knobs, pulls, escutcheons, electric plates, etc. Lower light fixtures from the ceilings and walls, or cover them with plastic that is firmly held in place with masking tape.

Dust the walls thoroughly with a dry mop or, better, a vacuum cleaner. Kitchen and bathroom walls and ceilings as well as other walls and ceilings that are very soiled should be washed with a detergent solution or commercial wall-cleaning compound. Pay particular attention to the baseboards and the tops of window and door frames, for these usually collect considerable dust and grease. Baseboards should also be scrubbed with coarse steel wool and then washed with benzine to take off floor wax that has accumulated over the paint.

Unless the floor is to be sanded and refinished, protect it from paint splatters with drop cloths. Or cover the entire floor with building paper that is held in place with masking tape.

Remove loose or peeling paint from woodwork and prime the exposed wood. Rough spots should be sanded smooth. If the existing paint is very hard and glossy, wipe with sandpaper or steel wool to cut the gloss so that the new paint will make a good bond.

NEW WORK   If surfaces have not been previously painted, sand smooth any rough spots on walls, ceilings, and woodwork. Fill holes with spackle. Coat all knots in softwood with a knot sealer. Prime woodwork with a suitable primer, and after it is dry, fill holes with spackle.

CEILINGS   If paint is to be applied by roller and the ceiling is not too high, use a roller with an extension handle. This will eliminate working from a stepladder. A ladder will be needed, however, to do the edges of the ceiling, which can't be done with a large roller. Do these areas with a small brush or edging pad. If paint is to be applied by brush or if the ceiling is very high, rent two stepladders with a plank to run between them.

When painting a ceiling work across the width, rather than the length of the room. If you use a fast-drying paint, never apply a strip wider than two feet. If the strip is too wide, the paint will begin to set before the next strip is applied and there will be lap marks.

WALLS   Start at the upper left-hand corner and work down towards the floor. If you are left handed, work from right to left. When applying paint with a roller, a long extension handle allows you to do the entire wall without a stepladder except for cutting in the corners between the walls and the ceiling.

Plaster   Small holes up to about ¼-inch diameter and hairline cracks in plaster walls and ceilings can be filled with spackle. Just clean out loose matter and smear the spackle in. Sand when dry.

PATCHING   For large holes and cracks, use patching plaster. This is mixed into a paste by adding water. Plaster of Paris can also be used but hardens very quickly.

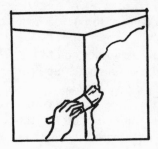

Paint corners and seams between walls and ceiling with a brush or special corner roller before attempting to use the roller on the rest of the surface.

Before applying patching plaster, remove loose plaster from the hole and undercut the edges so that they are wider inside than in front. This holds the patch in place. Cracks should also be cut out to allow the patching plaster to penetrate. Dampen the edges of the plaster before you trowel the patch into the hole and smooth it down.

Fill large holes in two coats. The first should come to within ¼ inch or so of the surface. Build the second on top of this when it has set.

Because of movement of the house framework, some cracks reappear even when properly patched. If this happens too often, try reinforcing the patch by smoothing a strip of gypsum-board tape into it.

PREPARING FOR PAINTING   New plaster walls and ceilings can be painted with latex or other water-emulsion paint as soon as they are dry. But if you intend to use an alkyd or other solvent-based paint, you must wait six months.

Whether plaster has been previously painted or not, before new paint is applied it should be free of grease, pencil marks, ink stains, and other difficult soil. Patched areas require two or three coats of paint to conceal them.

Gypsum board   This material is also known as dry wall and sheetrock. It comes in large sheets and consists of a core of gypsum plaster covered on both sides with heavy paper. It is used extensively for interior walls and ceilings. With a few exceptions, it can be painted in the same manner as plaster.

NEW WORK   Before painting, inspect the surface and correct any imperfections. Main points to check are the seams between panels and the cement over nail heads. Seams are covered by

applying a thin layer of gypsum-board cement, bedding a special paper tape in this, and then applying three additional layers
of cement. Nail heads should be set so that they dent but do not
break the paper covering, and are then covered with joint cement or spackle. If the work was not done properly in the first
place, apply one or two additional coats of cement and sand
smooth when dry.

Dust the entire wall or ceiling surface thoroughly and roll on
a latex primer-sealer. This is superior to a solvent-thinned primer
and will not raise the fibers on the paper covering. Follow with
one or two coats of latex flat wall-paint or, in kitchens and
bathrooms, a semi-gloss alkyd wall-paint.

OLD WORK   Wash walls and ceilings as necessary. Sand down
rough spots and fill holes and cracks with spackle. If nails have
popped out from the board, hammer them in and drive a second
nail alongside. Cover the heads with spackle or gypsum-board
cement. Roll on one or two coats of latex or alkyd wall paint.

Wallpaper   It is not advisable to paint wallpaper because it
makes later removal of the paper very difficult. Furthermore,
wallpaper is often not too well attached, and the weight of a

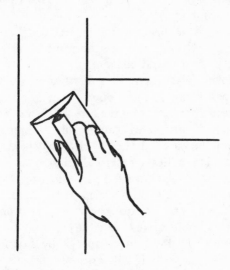

Always sand rough areas before painting.

coat of paint may pull it loose. If the wallpaper is in poor condition, it can take as much time to ready the surface for paint as it does to remove the paper. The dyes used in the patterns of some papers will bleed through various paints.

The one situation in which it is necessary to paint over wallpaper is when the paper has been applied to gypsum board that was not sized beforehand. To remove the wallpaper might damage the wallboard.

PREPARING WALLPAPER FOR PAINT   Clean the paper well. A light dusting may be sufficient, but in the case of a kitchen or bathroom, the paper should be washed to remove all traces of grease. Use a household-detergent solution on washable paper. On non-washable paper, you can use a dough-like wallpaper cleaner plus cleaning fluid for tough stains; but complete removal of the paper is advisable.

Split blisters in the paper with a razor blade and work paste underneath with a small spatula or knife. Press the paper back into place and allow the paste to dry. Loose edges of paper must also be pasted down. Small holes left by picture hooks can be filled with spackle. If the paper has been applied with a lap joint, the joints should be sanded well to make them as inconspicuous as possible.

About a week before painting, test whether the dyes in the wallpaper will bleed through the paint. Generally, you can use either a latex or alkyd wall paint.

REMOVING WALLPAPER   The best way to do this job is with a wallpaper steamer, which you can rent from tool-rental outlets. The steamer consists of a tank in which water is boiled, a long hose, and a perforated pan or plate through which steam emerges. The water is heated by electricity or kerosene.

To operate a steamer, start the heater and when steam has formed, move the perforated pan across the paper. Start at the bottom of the wall and work up. Hold the pan in place for 30 seconds or so until the paper can be peeled off easily in strips. Use a broad putty knife to ease the paper off the wall.

Another way to remove paper is by soaking it with warm water until the paste is soft. This job can be speeded by adding to the water a wallpaper remover designed to cut through the paper. The mixture can be applied to the wall with a sponge or brush, but the best tool is either a garden or a paint sprayer. Apply the liquid to an entire vertical section and then peel off the paper with a broad putty-knife. Be careful not to gouge the plaster or wallboard. If the paper does not come off readily, use more water.

When there are several layers of paper, remove one at a time. If the paper has been painted or is coated with plastic to make it washable, go over it with coarse sandpaper so it will absorb water.

Use drop cloths to protect the floor while removing wallpaper. Collect the wallpaper, as you rip it off, in a large container; it may stick to whatever it lands on otherwise.

After the paper is off, wash the wall thoroughly with water to get off lingering paste. Sand rough areas. Then apply a latex or alkyd primer followed by one or two finish coats.

Insulation board   This is also known as fiberboard and wallboard. Made from wood, sugar cane, or other vegetable fibers, the boards are used on interior walls and ceilings.

Insulation board is quite porous, so much of the material used in the house will have a factory-applied sealer. But it is hard to tell from casual examination whether your particular boards are sealed. The only way to make an accurate test is to apply a coat of primer sealer. If this dries to a uniform surface, the board is sealed. If the surface is not uniform, a second-seal coat is needed. After complete sealing, apply one or two coats of any good interior wall-paint.

When insulation board is used as a ceiling material in conjunction with exposed beams, it is customary to stain or varnish the beams before the ceiling is painted. This is done because it is easier to cut in the edges on the horizontal surfaces than on a vertical surface. When repainting the ceiling, masking tape should be applied along the edges of the beams where they join the insulation board to prevent getting paint on them.

Woodwork   If the woodwork in your house seems to need refinishing more often than the walls, it is simply because it receives more abuse. It is touched by dirty, oily hands; scarred by rings, shoes, toys and kiddie cars; exposed to dust and grease, which builds up on horizontal surfaces; soaked by moisture coming through or dripping off windows; and washed frequently.

Obviously, woodwork needs a durable finish, and of all those that can be used, the best are alkyd semi-gloss enamel (gloss enamel is even better but is too shiny) and satin-sheen urethane varnish.

Woodwork that is to be finished for the first time should be sanded smooth and clean. Spot-prime knots with a knot sealer. Fill holes and cracks in wood that is to be given a clear finish with plastic wood, and apply an oil stain of the desired color. Holes in wood that is to be painted should not be filled until after the wood is primed; then use spackle.

For an overall primer under a clear finish, use white shellac. Under enamel, use orange shellac; an alcohol-based, white-pigmented stain killer; or an alkyd primer. (If shellac or stain killer is used as the primer, earlier spot-priming of knots is unnecessary.)

Two coats of varnish or enamel will complete the job.

Woodwork that has been previously finished must be washed thoroughly with detergent solution and rinsed. Take care to remove floor wax from baseboards and the bottoms of doors. If the detergent doesn't touch this, scrub it with steel wool and then benzine. Sand scarred areas smooth. Fill holes. If the old finish is hard and glossy, go over it with steel wool or sandpaper to assure adhesion of the new finish. Finally, brush on alkyd enamel or urethane varnish.

Cornices If possible, these should be taken down from the walls before they are finished. Use the same paint or clear finish that is on other woodwork in the room.

Some people do not finish cornices on the inside on the theory that the bare wood cannot be seen. There is nothing wrong with this if the wood actually is invisible from all normal viewing angles. But note that, if a light is mounted inside a cornice, the inside surfaces should be painted white; otherwise the light reflected from them onto the wall below will be brownish, and the color of the wall will accordingly be distorted.

Doors Interior doors should be painted with an interior gloss or semi-gloss enamel; never a flat paint. Outside doors should be painted with an exterior-trim enamel. Use a brush to paint louvered and paneled doors. A roller can be used on flush doors. A roller can also be used to cover the large flat surfaces on a paneled door, but you must finish up with a brush.

If the old finish is in poor condition and must be removed, take the door down so it can be laid horizontally on a workbench or sawhorses.

Before painting a door, remove the knobs, escutcheons, and other surface-mounted hardware. Hinges are not removed, but care should be taken to keep paint off those made of solid brass Other hinges are often painted because they are likely to turn dull, lose their finish, and even start rusting.

Do the edges of the door first. Then, if it is a paneled door, paint the moldings and panels around them. Work from the top down. Do the raised surfaces last.

On panel doors, paint molding edges first, then paint entire panel.

When painting an exterior door for the first time, take it down and paint the top and bottom edges so they won't absorb moisture, which will cause the door to stick or warp.

See also garage doors.

Windows Use an interior-trim paint or spar varnish on the inside surfaces of windows and an exterior-trim enamel on any surface that is exposed to the weather.

Most wood windows require paint, inside and out, for protection as well as looks. The exceptions are units that come with a clear wood-sealer and require paint only for decorative purposes.

Steel windows must be kept well painted to prevent rust. Aluminum windows are usually painted only for decorative purposes, although paint or lacquer is often applied to prevent development of an unattractive oxide.

The best tool for painting a window is a good sash brush. The angular brush is probably the easiest to work with, but use any shape you like. There are also various special paint applicators, designed for making painting easier. You might try these if you find a brush difficult to handle.

The main problem in painting a sash is to keep the paint off the glass. One way to do this is to apply masking tape around the edges of each pane. The tape should butt against the frame but should not cover any part of it. To apply the tape properly calls for time and patience and is usually not worth the effort.

There are also metal and plastic shields that can be held against the frame to keep paint off the glass. These are satisfactory, although it is hard to keep some paint from leaking under the edges on to the glass.

If you have a good brush and exercise a little care, it is possible to paint the muntins without getting much, if any, paint on the glass. What does get on can be wiped off when wet or scraped off when dry with a single-edge razor blade. Many amateurs have found that it takes less time to scrape paint off glass than to take all the steps necessary to keep it off in the first place.

PREPARING WINDOWS FOR PAINTING Check joints between frames and walls and, if they are open, fill them with caulking compound. If the putty holding the glass in the frame is broken or missing, dig it out completely with a putty knife or chisel. Blow away dirt. If the frame is made of wood, you must then prime it with house paint or a thin coating of linseed oil.

Use either an oil or elastic putty. Because the latter remains elastic to some extent for many years, it helps to keep the glass from cracking when you slam down the window. On the other hand, it hardens so slowly that you won't be able to paint over it easily for a long time without denting the surface. Oil putty, on the other hand, hardens sufficiently for easy painting in a fortnight.

A special metal putty is used on steel and aluminum windows.

Sand or scrape off loose exterior and interior finish. In kitchens, bathrooms, and other humid areas, paint and varnish applied to window frames deteriorates rapidly, and much laborious scraping is called for to prepare the surface for a new finish. Be sure to let wood that has been water-soaked dry out completely before painting.

Remove rust on steel sash with sandpaper, and prime the bare metal with red lead.

PAINTING DOUBLE-HUNG WINDOWS There is a special sequence to painting these windows that should be followed to insure that all surfaces are covered.

First, raise the lower sash as far as it will go and pull down the upper sash halfway. Paint the muntins on the upper sash, and then paint the horizontal parts of the frame. Be sure that the bottom and top edges of these pieces are painted. Next, do the sides of the frame. Be careful not to use too much paint on these areas because if it runs into the joint between sash and the window frame, you may have a sticking window to contend with. After the upper sash has been completed, raise it almost to the top and check to see if there are any areas that have not been painted. Now lower the bottom sash and paint in the same sequence.

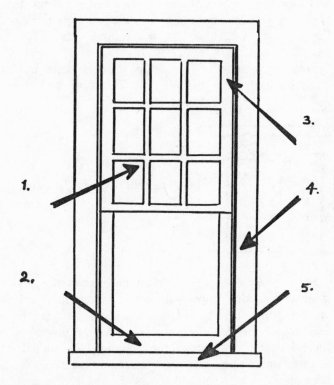

The correct method of painting a double hung window: 1. Paint the muntins. 2. Paint horizontals of sash. 3. Paint verticals of sash. 4. Paint verticals of frame. 5. Paint horizontal of frame and sill.

Use a rather dry brush when painting the sides of the sash and the inside of the frame. Too much paint in these areas will make the sash stick when the paint is dry.

Next, do the frame and casing. Start at the top, then do the sides, and end at the sill and apron underneath.

PAINTING CASEMENTS   These windows swing on hinges. Open them for painting. Paint the muntins first, then the top and bottom edges of the sash, then the sides and vertical edges, then the top and bottom of the frame, and, finally, the frame around the window.

Most casement windows are opened and closed by various kinds of cranks, arms, and adjusters. Take care not to get paint into the moving parts of these units.

On casement windows, paint the top and bottom edges first.

Windowsills   No paint or clear finish is overly good on a windowsill because most sills are under constant attack by moisture, dirt, and polluted air; as a result, even the toughest finish soon begins to deteriorate. It follows that unless you cover your windowsills with something more durable—laminated plastic or ceramic tile, for instance—you can expect to refinish them fairly often.

Wash with detergent solution and rinse well to start with. Let the sill dry thoroughly (it may have soaked up considerable water even before you washed it). Sand hard to remove rough and loose paint. Fill holes and sand again. Then brush on a couple of coats of the same finish that is used on the windows.

Baseboards The easiest part of finishing baseboards is to select the finish. Just use the same solvent-base semi-gloss enamel or clear finish that is applied to other woodwork in the room.

The hardest part of this paint job is to prepare old baseboards. This is because baseboards receive considerable abuse, which scars the finish; and in the course of time, they normally become splattered with floor wax. This must be removed completely before a new finish is applied. Alternately scrub with benzine and rub with steel wool.

Scars in the old finish should be removed by sanding. In an old house, you may well find that so many coats of paint have been applied that the only way you can eradicate the scars is to strip off all the paint with a chemical remover or electric paint-scraper.

For many people, the second most difficult job in painting baseboards is to keep the paint off the walls above and the floor below. If you find this a problem, too, the best solution is to stick masking tape to the walls and floor, right against the edges of the baseboard. Another solution is to hold a piece of thin cardboard or flat metal against the edge of the baseboard as you brush on paint. However, unless you wipe off the shield after every paint stroke, you will find to your regret that paint curling around the lower edge leaves a blot on the wall or floor behind.

Stairs If stairs are to be painted use a floor and deck enamel. Do not use ordinary paints because they will not hold up for

Use a metal or cardboard shield when painting baseboards to keep paint off floor and walls.

long. Stairs may also be finished with varnish or penetrating floor-sealer.

Clean stairs thoroughly before refinishing. Use a prepared paint cleaner or solvent to remove all traces of dirt and heel marks. Sand rough spots on treads and risers.

Painting stairs does not present much of a problem if there are two flights in the house so that one can be out of service. But if there is only one flight of stairs, you will have to take one of several approaches to keep the stairs in service during the day. One approach is to paint every other tread and riser. When these are dry, paint the alternate treads and riser. This is only practical when the individuals using the stairs have long legs.

Another approach is to paint half the width of the stairs, and when that side is dry, paint the other side. Still another approach is to paint the stairs at night with a fast-drying floor enamel. Start from the bottom and work up. In the morning, cover the treads with sheets of wax paper so that even if the paint is not completely dry, it will not be damaged by shoes. The wax paper lifts off easily when the paint is dry.

These methods can also be used when varnish or floor sealer is to be applied. If you use shellac rather than these clear finishes, it will, of course, dry in a couple of hours, but it will not wear as well.

Railings on stairs can be painted either with a semigloss or gloss enamel, spar varnish, or several thin coats of white shellac.

Acoustical tile   To keep the paint from interfering with the sound-absorbing value of acoustical tile, apply as thin a coat as is required to give coverage. The best type of paint is a casein or interior oil-paint. Latex paint may be used but tends to fill in the holes in the tile, so you must clear the holes with a toothpick before the paint dries.

Tile should be cleaned before painting. This is especially important in the kitchen, where the ceiling is usually coated with grease.

Spraying is the best way to paint acoustical tile because it produces the thinnest coating of paint. A brush or roller may also be used. *See* insulation board.

Bathrooms   Paints for these heavy-duty areas must be designed to resist damage from moisture, soap and medicines, and must withstand frequent washing. The most popular choices are the gloss or semi-gloss alkyd enamels because of their washability and resistance to moisture. Latex paint also resists moisture but is less washable.

Before painting a bathroom, remove wall fixtures and other accessories. Wash all surfaces to be painted with household detergent, and sand lightly to roughen them. Cover plumbing fixtures with drop cloths. Check the condition of the caulking between a recessed bathtub and the wall, and replace it if in poor condition.

Bedrooms *See* house, interior. Instead of conventional finishes, fire-retardant paints are sometimes used in bedrooms occupied by infants, elderly persons, and invalids.

Burlap Burlap is sometimes used to cover walls. If you want to paint it either to give it a color or to make it more resistant to soiling, you can apply any interior wall paint you like. But at least three and probably four coats will be required for a uniform coverage. Apply with a spray gun or brush. A roller can also be used but is not suitable for the first coat because you can't force the finish into the weave.

You should, of course, make sure the burlap is stuck tightly to the wall before painting it.

Closets Since most closets don't have enough light, it is best to paint the interior white or as light a color as will fit into your decorating scheme. A flat wall-paint is adequate for the walls, but shelves should be painted with an enamel so they will be easy to wipe clean. Wood closet-poles should also be coated with an enamel.

If the finish on brass hooks is in good condition, remove them before painting the closet. But if the finish has worn off, you will save time and come up with a better-looking closet interior if you paint the hooks with the same paint as used on the shelves.

Closets are poorly ventilated, so when you paint them, aim an electric fan into them to keep the air circulating and prevent the possibility of being harmed by the paint fumes.

Grasscloth This is pasted to walls like wallpaper. If the material is secure, it can be painted with any interior wall paint. Because the cloth is very absorbent, at least three coats will be necessary for uniform coverage.

Hardware   Hardware interferes with the painting of doors, windows, baseboards, etc., and sometimes needs refinishing itself.

While it is impractical to remove all hardware when painting a room, it is a smart idea to take the time to remove as much as possible. This is especially true of items that should not be painted, such as door knobs; items that are hard to paint around, such as window catches; and items that will become scarred if you paint over them, such as strikeplates in door jambs. To prevent loss of hardware and screws you remove, put all pieces for each room together in a can or dish.

If you don't think your painting hand is very steady, cover hardware items that you don't remove with masking tape.

Hardware to be painted should be wiped clean with a detergent solution and then with clear water. While the metal may be too highly polished to hold paint well, don't roughen it with steel wool because you may some day want to return to the metal finish. Apply a solvent-base gloss or semi-gloss enamel on interior hardware and a gloss enamel made for metal on exterior hardware.

If metal, such as solid brass, is to be left natural, remove all tarnish and old lacquer. Then spray on several coats of clear lacquer.

Kitchens   Because kitchens require a finish that will not catch and hold dirt and grease, and that will stand up under repeated washing, the best choice of paint is an alkyd semi-gloss or gloss interior-enamel. Latex paints are not recommended because they require several weeks to age before they are washable; and even then they never are very easy to wash.

Painting a new kitchen is similar to painting any other new room. In the case of an existing kitchen, it is essential that all surfaces be thoroughly cleaned to remove dirt and grease. Use a strong detergent solution, work on small sections, scrub hard and rinse well.

Thresholds   Thresholds at exterior doors receive very hard wear from traffic and are, in addition, under constant attack by sun, rain, and blowing sand and dirt. Because of this, they need to be refinished once a year, and in many cases, more often.

If kept in reasonably good shape, a threshold needs only to

be wiped clean with turpentine or benzine and sanded well. The most durable finish is a high-quality deck enamel. For a less durable clear-finish, use marine spar varnish. Apply two coats of both.

If the old finish on a threshold has been allowed to deteriorate, you will probably have to fill cracks with plastic wood. You may also have to bleach the wood if you plan to use a clear finish.

Interior thresholds are finished like wood floors.

Vinyl fabrics To paint vinyl fabric that is hung like wallpaper, paste down loose strips with vinyl adhesive. If blisters are present, slit them with a sharp knife and spread adhesive underneath with a small spatula. After all repairs are made, clean the wall covering with household detergent solution. Grease, oil, lipstick, and other stains that do not come off should be removed with mineral spirits.

If the fabric is smooth and without a design, use an alkyd flat wall-paint as the primer. When dry, apply one or two finish coats of alkyd or latex paint. As a rule, latex is used for a flat finish and alkyd for a semi-gloss finish.

If the fabric has a design, prime it with a latex primer-sealer. This is essential to prevent the design from bleeding through the finish coat of paint. For the finish coats, use latex or alkyd wall-paint.

On textured fabrics, use an oil-based primer sealer or an alkyd flat paint. Finish with an alkyd flat or enamel.

To paint flexible vinyl fabrics used for upholstery, accordion doors, motorcycle seats, etc., wash the fabric and dry. Then apply one of the special vinyl fabric spray-paints that are available in aerosol cans.

Wood paneling If the wall is going to be exposed to rather hard wear and frequent cleaning, as in a family room, finish it in the way described under woodwork. In less vulnerable areas, however, you can get by very well with a less durable, more easily applied finish. A good one is stain wax (*see* stain waxes). Another is made by applying an oil stain, overcoating it with a thin coat of white shellac, and finishing with a coat of wax.

Whatever the finish used, it is extremely important that you stain the paneling or apply the first finish coat of paint before the wall is built. Take pains to cover the edges of the panels as well as the face. The reason for this is that much of the wood sold today is inadequately seasoned; consequently, if you don't color the panel edges before installation, the bare wood will be exposed when the panels shrink.

how to paint and refinish wood and concrete floors

WOOD FLOORS   The quick and easy way to refinish a wood floor is to paint it. But unfortunately, this is also the least successful way because even the best paint does not wear well underfoot.

The first step is to remove all wax that has been applied. Scrub first with coarse steel-wool; then wash with benzine to remove the residue.

Nail down loose and squeaky boards. Countersink protruding nails. Fill cracks and holes with plastic wood. Remove peeling or chipped finish with paint remover or by hand sanding. Sand all other scratched and rough areas smooth.

Apply two coats of latex or alkyd floor enamel according to the maker's directions. Generally, with alkyd the first coat should be thinned with about a pint of thinner to a gallon of enamel. Apply the second coat straight from the can. When using latex, apply both coats from the can. The advantage of latex, of course, is that it's fast drying.

SANDING WOOD FLOORS   There are very few wood floors that do not show off to better advantage under a clear finish than under paint. They also wear better.

The most practical way to prepare a floor for a clear finish is by sanding. This not only removes old paint, varnish, and shellac but also eradicates many stains, leaving the wood satin-smooth and ready for staining and finishing.

Floors are sanded with power floor-sanders, which can be rented by the day from paint, hardware, and tool-rental stores. Two types of machines are required. One is a large drum-sander; the other a small rotary sander called an edger. Areas that can't be reached with the edger must be done with a hand

When painting a floor, paint in strips about two feet wide and paint in the direction of the wood grain.

scraper, sandpaper, or steel wool. When sanders are rented, the necessary amount of sandpaper will be supplied. Three grades will be required: coarse, medium, and fine. Before you take the equipment, have the clerk explain the operation of each machine and how the sandpaper is installed.

All furniture, window shades, draperies, and pictures should be removed from the room before you begin sanding. In spite of the fact that sanders are equipped with bags to catch the dust, a considerable amount of fine dust will escape. Close the doors and open the windows.

Check the floor carefully before sanding. If any nail heads protrude above the surface, drive them in with a nailset. If you don't do this, they will rip the sandpaper to shreds.

The first sanding operation is done with the drum sander fitted with coarse paper. Retract the sanding drum so that it is not in contact with the floor, start the motor and gently lower the drum, while at the same time moving the machine slowly across the floor. Never allow the sanding drum (or wheel on the edger) to be in contact with the floor when the sander is not being moved because it will cut a depression into the floor in seconds.

Unless the floor is very rough and uneven, sand in the direction of the grain. If the floor is very rough, the first cut can be made across the grain, but all subsequent cuts must be made with the grain.

Use the drum sander to do as much of the floor as possible, and then use the edger with coarse paper to finish those areas that were missed. Repeat this process with the medium paper in both machines and then with the fine paper. Remove the old finish in corners, around pipes, and in other hard-to-get-at places by hand. Before the final sanding, it is wise to remove your shoes or slip a pair of old socks over your shoes so that you won't mark up the bare wood.

Stains in the wood that do not respond to sanding can be removed by bleaching (*see* bleaching wood).

After the final sanding, give the room a thorough cleaning with your vacuum cleaner.

SANDING PARQUET FLOORS   Parquet floors are extremely difficult to sand because the grain of alternate blocks runs in different directions. You will therefore be well advised to hire a professional floor sander.

If you do the work yourself, make only two cuts—first with medium and then with fine sandpaper. The first cut can be made with a drum sander, but the final cut over the entire floor must be made with a rotary sander using No. oo paper. For good measure, you should then go over the floor on hands and knees, touching up individual blocks by hand.

APPLYING THE FINISH   The pores in oak and other open-grained woods may be filled with paste wood-filler after staining, but there are relatively few people who bother to do this.

Whether you stain the wood depends on the effect you wish to achieve. Generally an oil stain is used, but there are a few finishes that call for other types of stain. Apply the stain in long strips about 24 to 30 inches wide; and complete one strip before progressing to the next. Before starting the job, take note of the layout of the room so you won't work yourself into a corner from which you can't escape. (The same rule obviously applies when you apply the final finish.)

Apply the stain to the wood with a wide brush and spread it out as evenly as possible. Let it penetrate for a few minutes; then wipe off the excess with clean, dry cloths. If the color is not as deep as you want, make a second application. Make note of roughly how many minutes it takes from the first brushing-on to the final rubbing-off to achieve the desired color. Time all subsequent applications more or less in the same way.

After staining a strip of floor and blotting up the excess, go back over the strip once more and rub out lap marks. When the entire floor is done, allow it to dry for at least 24 hours.

In most homes, the most satisfactory floor finish is a penetrating floor-sealer. This sinks into the wood fibers and forms a wear-resistant surface. One of the sealer's greatest advantages is that when it becomes scratched you can touch it up without leaving any visible lap marks. It is the only finish recommended for maple floors, and its flexibility adapts it better than varnish to softwood floors.

Brush the first coat of sealer on across the grain and smooth out with the grain. Although some professional floor finishers use lamb's-wool applicators, this is a doubtful practice because it frequently results in coatings that are too thick and uneven. Apply an even film with your brush and wipe up the excess with rags, if the manufacturer's directions so specify. Then allow the sealer to dry completely. The time required varies with the brand.

You should then buff the entire floor with steel wool and take up the dust with a vacuum cleaner. Brush on (with the grain) a second coat of sealer and let it dry well before walking on the floor. If you find the shiny finish objectionable, rub it down lightly with fine steel wool. Finish with a coat of solvent-base wax.

A second type of finish often used on home floors is floor varnish. Urethane or a two-part varnish are particularly recommended because of their excellent resistance to wear, especially on hardwoods. When scratched, however, varnish is almost impossible to touch up without showing lap marks.

Apply two coats, 24 hours apart. Both should be brushed on with the grain. If you use a high-gloss varnish, go over the second coat, when dry, with fine steel-wool to subdue the shine.

Shellac and stain wax are also used to finish wood floors, but they do not wear so well as varnish or penetrating sealer. Both show water spots.

REFURBISHING AN OLD FINISH   If you do a good finishing job on wood floors in the first place, and maintain the finish with reasonable care, there is no reason why your floors should need complete refinishing for many, many years. The odds are, however, that they will need a bit of sprucing up from time to time.

This is a simple job if you have used penetrating sealer. Just remove the wax and sand the exposed sealer lightly to remove scratches. Take up the dust with a vacuum. If the wood is scratched, brush on a light coat of stain of the proper color. Then brush on one or two coats of sealer. When the last coat is dry, steel-wool lightly and apply wax.

Varnish is finished in the same way, but since it does not blend in with the old finish, the only way to avoid obvious lap marks in some situations is to refinish the floor from wall to wall.

Gym seal A penetrating floor sealer especially formulated for gymnasium floors. It is sometimes used in homes, especially on floors exposed to a lot of wear. *See* floor sealers.

CONCRETE FLOORS   New concrete floors should be allowed to cure for several months before they are painted. No floor should be painted if it is frequently damp.

The first step in finishing a floor is to scrub it with trisodium phosphate to remove dirt and grease.

An old floor that has been previously painted must be stripped down to the concrete, unless the finish is sound. Use a solution of 1 pound lye in 5 pints water. Wear rubber gloves and goggles. Apply with a long-handled brush and allow the solution to stand until the paint softens. Then scrape it off with a hoe followed by a stiffbrush. Several applications may be necessary to get up all spots.

Both old and new floors must be cleaned and etched with muriatic acid to open up the pores so the new paint will make a good bond. Dilute the acid with water to make a 20 percent solution (*see* muriatic acid) and apply it with a long-handled brush. Let it stand until it stops bubbling; then rinse thoroughly with clear water.

Finish the floor with a floor enamel that is specifically rec ommended for concrete. The paints available include epoxies, urethanes, latexes, oil-base alkyds, and solvent-thinned rubber-base enamels. Of these, the epoxies are the most durable. They are highly resistant to abrasion, sub-surface and surface moisture.

Solvent-thinned rubber-base enamels should not be used in garages and other areas where they will be exposed to gasoline and oil. Latex enamels do not stand up well in tire lanes on garage floors; and they should also not be used in situations where they will be exposed to moisture within 24 hours after application.

Oil-base alkyds should not be used on new concrete or concrete that becomes damp.

Unless you are using a latex enamel, allow the concrete to dry completely before painting. Latex can be applied to a damp surface.

Work with a wide brush or roller. For the first coat, a brush is the more desirable because it does a better job of working the paint into the pores of the concrete. A roller saves time on the second coat. Three coats are rarely necessary.

CLEAR FINISHES   The only purpose of a clear finish on concrete is to prevent excessive staining and make for easier cleaning. Use a colorless masonry sealer and apply two coats.

STAINING CONCRETE   *See* driveways.

Brick floors   Most bricks used in building are rather porous and readily stained. It follows that brick interior floors should be coated with a clear masonry sealer as soon as they are laid. Apply two coats and then apply self-polishing liquid wax.

Brick floors can, of course, be painted like concrete floors. But they are too handsome to be treated in such fashion. Furthermore, paint on brick is extremely difficult to remove, and you just might some day want to remove it.

Ceramic or quarry-tile floors   The only paint that will hold satisfactorily on these surfaces is an epoxy floor enamel. For how to apply it, *see* ceramic tile.

Cork floors   Remove wax with a prepared wax remover; then rinse, swab as dry as possible with a sponge, and allow to air-dry for 24 hours or more. Try to remove stains with detergent solution or benzine. If this fails, sand the cork carefully with medium and then fine sandpaper; but don't cut too deep.

If you want to stain cork, apply an oil stain. Then brush on two coats of a clear, penetrating floor-sealer. Allow 24 hours between coats. After the second coat has dried 24 hours, if it is objectionably shiny, dull it by rubbing with medium steel wool. Then wax.

Flagstone and slate floors   A finish is not essential but is desirable to make the stone more resistant to stains and easier to clean and wash. Apply two coats of a clear masonry sealer after dusting and, if necessary, washing the floor. Then apply a buffable liquid wax.

Garage floors Paints for these surfaces must resist wear and abrasion, moisture, alkalies, gasoline, and oil. The best are the epoxy and urethane concrete floor enamels. Nothing else is adequately durable. *See* floors, concrete.

Resilient floors You should never apply paint, varnish or any other hard, clear finish to resilient flooring, even though various products are recommended for the purpose. The reason is that the finish will soon wear out in traffic lanes. When this happens, you can apply a new coat of paint, but if you apply a clear finish, it will not match the old finish. Furthermore, if you ever try to remove the paint or clear finish, you will damage the flooring.

A water wax is the only finish that should ever be applied to linoleum, vinyl, asphalt tile, etc. However, if you absolutely insist on making your life miserable in the future, remove every speck of wax with a prepared wax remover, rinse, and dry well. For a clear finish, use one of the transparent sealers erroneously touted as miracle finishes for resilient floors. They are no good, but they are better than nothing. For an opaque finish, use an alkyd floor enamel.

Seamless floors These floors are made by pouring a plastic from a can and spreading it over the floor in an unbroken sheet. Once down, no finish—not even wax—is normally applied. But in time, when the floor becomes worn, it must be reglazed or, very occasionally, resurfaced. The work should be done by a professional.

how to paint and
refinish furniture

WOOD FURNITURE   Furniture should be finished in a warm, dry, well-ventilated room in which there is very little air movement and in which you have plenty of space to work. Vacuum the room thoroughly to capture all possible dust that might land on the furniture. Cover the floor with newspapers when using a chemical paint remover, and lay down fresh papers or dropcloths when applying the finish. If you plan to use a spray gun or aerosol, cover everything in the room that might come within the line of fire.

The actual finishing operation starts with the removal of all hardware from the furniture piece. Then take the piece apart as much as possible: remove drawers, seats, finials, and so forth.

APPLYING A PAINT FINISH   Obviously the easiest way to finish furniture is to paint it because you don't have to do a great deal of surface preparation. If you're working on unfinished furniture, smooth the wood with sandpaper or steel wool. If the wood has an open grain, thin paste wood-filler to the consistency of heavy varnish and brush it on across the grain and then with the grain. Let it dry for about a half hour, and wipe it off—across the grain—with rags. When the filler is completely dry, sand the wood again lightly.

For the first coat, apply enamel undercoater, orange shellac, or a pigmented shellac (generally called a stain kill). After this is dry, fill holes and cracks in the wood with spackle, and spot-prime these patches when dry. Then sand the entire piece lightly and apply two coats of solvent-base interior enamel. The alternative is to use lacquer.

Previously finished furniture should be washed well with detergent solution, rinsed and allowed to dry. If you suspect it has been polished, wash it with benzine, too. Repair loose joints, etc. If there are holes and cracks to be filled, prime any bare wood that is showing with shellac and then apply spackle. This should be coated with shellac when it is dry and has been sanded. Go over the entire furniture piece with sandpaper to feather edges around chipped spots in the old finish, smooth out lumps, and roughen the surface so it will hold paint. You can then apply enamel directly to the old finish, but you will get better results if you use an enamel undercoater tinted to the final color. In either case, a second coat of enamel is needed for perfect coverage.

Lacquer should not be used on previously finished furniture unless you first apply a prime coat of shellac. It may destroy the old finish otherwise.

APPLYING A CLEAR FINISH   If an old clear finish is sound but covered with tiny scratches, light alligatoring, and whitish marks, you may be able to save yourself a lot of work by trying to restore it. Wash with benzine to remove polish. Then lightly rub a small area with medium, followed by fine, steel wool to remove the top layer of finish. If the lower layer of finish is free of flaws and is presentable, you can then go over the entire furniture piece in the same way. When through, wash it once more with benzine, and apply one or two coats of white shellac or varnish.

If complete refinishing of furniture is required, your first step is to remove all the old finish down to the bare wood. This is most easily done with a paste-type chemical remover. Make whatever major repairs are necessary. Bleach the wood to remove stains or lighten the color all over. Fill holes and cracks with a shellac stick or plastic wood that is colored to match the final finish. Remove burn marks by sanding. If the depression this leaves is shallow, fill it in after the wood is stained by applying shellac in thin coats. When all this preliminary work is done, sand the entire piece until it is completely smooth and free of scratches. Start with medium sandpaper and progress to fine sandpaper or steel wool. The wood should feel like silk when you are finished.

Brush a coat of oil stain of the desired color on the wood and let it stand for a few minutes. Stain only a small section at a

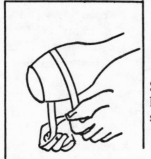

Sanding rounded surfaces, such as table legs and railings, is easy if you cut the sandpaper into thin strips.

time because the stain penetrates rapidly, especially if the wood is soft. Then wipe it off with clean rags. If the color is not deep enough, repeat the process. Keep track of how many minutes it takes between the first application of stain and the final wiping off. Then follow the same time schedule for succeeding applications. (This assumes that the entire furniture piece is made of the same wood. If it is made of two or more different woods, the time it takes for stain to penetrate will vary.)

After the entire piece has been stained, go over it once more with a clean rag to even out the stain. Let the stain dry for at least 24 hours before rubbing down the wood lightly, once more, with very fine steel wool.

Now fill open-grained woods with paste wood-filler, applying it in the way described above. Use a filler that is colored to match the stain. When it is dry, steel-wool all surfaces. You are now ready to apply the final finish.

There are many good ones to choose from. The following are recommended because they are relatively simple, yet beautiful. The most important thing to remember in applying the first two is that the furniture must be free of dust. Wipe it off thoroughly with a tack rag before each operation.

VARNISH FINISH This is the easiest of the three, provided you can control the dust.

Brush on a 3-pound cut of fresh white shellac. Sand with fine sandpaper or steel wool when dry. Then brush on one coat of water-clear varnish. You can use a flat varnish or, for a more durable film, a gloss varnish. To remove the objectionable shine from the latter, go over it with very fine steel-wool; then pumice and oil it.

DIP AND RUB FINISH   Brush on a mixture of 1 part white shellac (4-pound cut) and 2 parts turpentine. Smooth with fine sandpaper or steel wool when dry. Then fill one saucer with turpentine and another with 4-pound white shellac (uncut). Fold a piece of lint-free cloth into a pad; dip it in the turpentine, then in the shellac, and rub it on the wood with a rotary motion. When the entire piece has been treated, let the finish dry for three hours and repeat the process three more times. The finish should have a rich, soft gloss.

LINSEED-OIL FINISH   This takes quite a lot of work, but you don't have to worry about dust. The final finish has a deep, warm glow and does not need to be waxed. If it looks dull at any time, you can restore it quickly by rubbing with a few drops of linseed.

Heat boiled or raw linseed oil over water until it is quite warm, but not unpleasantly so. Pour some on the furniture piece, spreading it evenly over the surface and rubbing hard for about 20 minutes with a coarse rag. Then remove the excess with a clean rag. Proceed in this way, doing one section after another. Then let the oil dry for a week and make a second application in the same way. Most people stop after that; but you will achieve an even finer, more durable finish if you repeat the process one or two times more.

Stenciling   A stencil is a thin sheet of stiff cardboard or metal with a cutout design, letters, or numerals. It is used to paint the design accurately on a surface.

Many prepared stencils, particularly of letters and numerals, are available. You can also make your own stencils by drawing designs on stiff, oil-treated cardboard, like that often used for dividers in filing cabinets, and then cutting them out with a sharp knife or razor blade.

To transfer the design to a table top, for instance, set the stencil in position and smooth it tight to the table; then tape the edges down with masking tape so the stencil won't move.

Mix colors-in-oil with a little linseed oil in a saucer or pour a little enamel from a can into a saucer. Tap the bristle ends of a stencil brush (a small, round brush with short bristles) in the paint; then tap them straight down on the cutout part of the stencil. Do not brush sideways, lest you get paint under the edges of the stencil. When the cutout area is filled in, leave the stencil in place until the paint is quite dry. If you lift it off immediately, the chances are that the paint edges will run or be blurred.

SPECIAL PIECES OF FURNITURE   *Beds* Beds are best painted when they are assembled because you can cover the back, front, top and bottom of all surfaces at one time. But to complete the job, it may be necessary to take the beds apart when the paint is dry in order to paint the spots where the rails butt against the head and footboards.

Bookshelves Bookshelves and bookcases need a durable, washable finish because they collect dust and grease and receive considerable wear from books being pushed in and out. For a paint finish, a semi-gloss or gloss alkyd-enamel is recommended. For a clear finish, use urethane varnish.

Before making an application, wash all surfaces well with detergent solution or, if necessary, with a powdered cleanser. Rinse well and sand smooth.

Built-ins These are almost always made of wood, plywood, hardboard and/or particleboard, and are painted or given a clear finish like the interior woodwork in the same room. To prevent doors and drawers made of wood or plywood from binding in damp weather, it is advisable to seal the edges and hidden surfaces with a couple of coats of shellac or varnish. Hardboard and particleboard are so dense and stable that they do not need this treatment.

Chairs See wood furniture or metal furniture.

Remove padded seats on straight chairs if possible. Place the chair on a table or workbench; turn it upside down and do the bottom of the seat, the legs and back first. Then set the chair upright and do all other surfaces. Paint the top of the seat last. Aerosol paints or a painter's mitt are time-savers for doing rungs, legs, and other rounded surfaces. If you use a brush on rounded legs, rungs, etc., apply paint across the grain; then smooth it out with the grain.

Chest of drawers See wood furniture; also drawers. Take off hardware and knobs before starting work. Pull out drawers, set them face up, and apply paint. Paint the frame from the top down.

Chests Remove hardware, if any. Paint the top of the lid first. Then open it and paint the underside and the interior and exterior of the box. For an opaque finish, an alkyd enamel is generally the best choice. Use a furniture or spar varnish for a clear finish.

OUTDOOR FURNITURE, METAL

After being exposed to the weather for a period of time, aluminum will become discolored. To restore it to its original shiny condition and keep it that way, clean with a phosphoric acid cleaner and then polish the metal with fine steel wool until it is bright. Wipe clean with a paint thinner and coat with a clear non-yellowing acrylic lacquer. If the lacquer is applied to new aluminum furniture after it has been wiped with a solvent, the bright surface will not become discolored.

To paint aluminum outdoor furniture, clean the metal well and apply a wood or metal primer that has a high zinc content. Follow with two coats of exterior enamel.

Cast-iron and steel furniture must be kept covered with paint at all times. You should examine it carefully every spring. Usually it's a good idea to apply another coat of enamel at that time even if the old surface is in pretty good shape.

Before painting, wash the furniture with detergent solution and sand it to reduce the gloss of the old finish. Remove rust and prime the bare metal with a metal primer. Then brush or spray on a gloss enamel made for metal.

Chrome furniture is kept in condition by going over it in the spring with a chrome cleaner and protector available at auto supply stores. If the chrome is broken and the base metal starts to rust, remove the rust; prime, and apply a chrome-finish aluminum paint.

OUTDOOR FURNITURE: WOOD, BAMBOO, RATTAN, WICKER

Redwood furniture is often left unfinished, only to become dirty and stained. It should really be finished like all other outdoor furniture made of wood or wood-like materials

For a paint finish, apply an alkyd primer and overcoat with

alkyd trim paint. Apply two coats of spar varnish for a clear finish. If you object to the high gloss, rub carefully with fine steel wool.

Varnished outdoor furniture that is exposed to the weather needs to be refinished every spring, because the combination of sun, rain, and heat causes rapid deterioration; and when the protective film disappears, the wood underneath is likely to become discolored.

METAL FURNITURE   Chrome needs no finishing but should be gone over occasionally with a chrome cleaner and protector.

Protect brass-plated steel by spraying with a clear lacquer. If the film is chipped, remove the entire coating with lacquer thinner and respray. Unfortunately, if the plate itself wears off, the only way to restore it is to take the piece to a metal-plating shop. You can, however, change the color by spraying it with a pigmented lacquer.

Painted steel and wrought iron are repainted with a solvent-base interior gloss-enamel or with enamel made for metal.

For how to finish aluminum, *see* outdoor furniture, aluminum.

PLASTIC FURNITURE   The plastics most commonly used in furniture today are difficult to identify as plastics. They are cleverly colored, textured, and "carved" to resemble wood, and are then usually combined with real wood in such things as chests, chairs, and beds. The only way you can detect the fake wood is to examine it close-up and even cut into it with a knife.

Wood-resembling plastics of this type are finished at the factory with the same clear finish used on the real wood. If and when the finish needs to be done over, proceed as with wood furniture. Just do not let paint remover stand very long on the plastics.

The plastics can also be painted, like wood, with enamel.

Other furniture—usually of modern or contemporary design —is more obviously made of plastics. These may be clear or colored, reinforced with fiberglass, or laminated.

As long as any of these plastics are rigid, they can be painted. Just wash thoroughly and roughen with coarse steel wool. Then apply a solvent-base primer and compatible enamel.

REED, WICKER, RATTAN, OR BAMBOO FURNITURE

For a colored finish, follow directions for enameling wood furniture.

For a durable natural finish, apply two coats of varnish or a coat of white shellac followed by a coat of varnish. Wicker can be stained before the varnish is applied; but the other materials generally are too dense to absorb stain.

Old pieces of furniture must be dusted and washed—preferably under a hose—to remove soil. But removal of an old finish is usually too difficult to be attempted. About the only thing you can do (and then only on strips of large diameter) is to scrape off very poor finish with a knife and sand with medium sandpaper. Small stained areas can be bleached with oxalic acid.

Countertops and bars, wood   For a clear finish, use a so-called bar varnish, which is designed to be liquid and alcohol resistant. If an opaque finish is desired, the most durable is an epoxy or urethane enamel.

Cushions, canvas   If they have not been waterproofed, paint these with a canvas paint. Clean thoroughly before painting. *See* canvas.

Desks   *See* wood furniture; metal furniture; drawers. Take off hardware and knobs. Remove the drawers and set them upright in order to paint the front surface. Paint the frame from the top down.

Drawers   Drawers from bureaus, desks, built-ins, kitchen cabinets, etc. should be removed from their frames and placed face up for quick, easy painting. Preparation of the surface and selection of finish are covered under wood furniture or metal furniture.

If wood drawers have a tendency to stick in warm, damp weather, wait until they shrink in winter and then brush a couple of coats of shellac or varnish on the inner surfaces and backs of the sides, back panel, and bottom. This will help to seal out moisture and prevent further sticking.

Swollen wood can also be shrunk at any time of the year by burning a 100-watt incandescent bulb inside a closed drawer. Be sure to set the bulb on an insulated pad of some sort to prevent charring of the drawer bottom.

Knobs and pulls Always remove these when refinishing doors, cabinets, or chests. Not even a professional can work around them without getting some paint on them.

Do not apply any finish to glass, plastic, or porcelain knobs: it may stick at the start but will soon wear off.

The most durable paint finish for metal knobs, escutcheons, pulls, and so forth is two coats of epoxy enamel. For a clear finish use two or three thin coats of lacquer.

Wipe the knobs and pulls clean with detergent solution, benzine, or turpentine. If they are covered with lacquer that has begun to peel, remove all that remains with lacquer thinner. Paint or any other finish that is in bad repair or has been splattered on the knobs should be removed by dipping in paint remover and rubbing with a soft cloth. Do not scrape off paint with a knife because you will scratch the metal.

Place the knobs and pulls on wax paper and apply the finish with a brush or, much better, a spray can. Don't try too hard to cover the pieces entirely at one time. You will avoid sloppy workmanship if you let the pieces dry, then set them in several new positions and paint them again and again until they are completely covered. Use masking tape on parts of knobs that should not be painted.

Screw heads should be painted, too, but make sure the slots are clean before you do so. Hold the screws in your fingers, paint them with a brush, and place them on wax paper to dry.

Sideboards Finish like a chest of drawers (*see* wood furniture).

Tables Turn a table upside down and do the legs and bottom first. Then turn the table upright and paint the top and edges (*see* wood and metal furniture).

CHILDREN'S FURNITURE   Children's furniture is usually made of wood and is finished like your own furniture (*see* wood furniture). But there is one important thing to remember: whatever enamel you use must be free of lead.

A varnish finish will prove to be the most durable clear finish. (For extra protection, apply two coats of varnish over a base coat of shellac. Urethane varnish is particularly tough.) On the other hand, the inevitable scars are impossible to patch so they are invisible. For this reason a less durable, more easily repaired shellac finish may strike you as more desirable. Simply apply a well-thinned first coat; and follow with two coats of 3-pound cut shellac. Sand lightly between all coats.

Cribs Like beds, cribs are most easily painted or varnished when they are assembled; but it may be necessary to take them apart to cover the spots where the sides butt against the head and footboards. If you use paint on a crib, it must not contain lead. *See* wood furniture.

Playpens Scrape off stuck-on food with a knife; wash with detergent solution and rinse; then sand as necessary. Apply one or two coats of gloss or semi-gloss *lead-free* alkyd enamel.

If you use a painter's mitt to paint the sides you'll probably achieve more complete coverage in a shorter time. But before the paint becomes tacky, smooth off each upright and rail with lengthwise strokes of a brush.

14

special finishes for furniture and woodwork

There are a wide variety of special finishes. Most of them are designed primarily for use on furniture and interior woodwork, although there are some, such as the stippled finish, that are used on interior walls.

Some of these special finishes are very easy to apply, but others will require considerable time, attention to detail, and skill. Before attempting to do a large piece of work with some of the more complex finishes, it is wise to try it out on a practice surface to see if the time and effort involved are worth the final result.

Antique finishes These are very popular for furniture and wood paneling. They consist of a basecoat of paint—either white or colored—over which is applied a semi-transparent glaze that is wiped or brushed before dry to produce various shading effects. Often a second color is applied to moldings, trim or scrollwork to highlight these areas before the glaze is applied.

The necessary materials for antiquing are available in kit form; but the same results can be obtained by using a satin-finish enamel for the base, and second color and a glazing liquid for the finish coat.

Antique finishes are used on new work as well as over surfaces that have been previously painted. If the old paint is in good condition, it need only be cleaned with a detergent solution. Sand lightly to cut the gloss. If the old paint is in poor condition, it should be taken off with a paint remover. Sand the wood smooth and prime it before applying the basecoat.

Brush on the basecoat and allow it to dry. Sand with fine finishing paper, and then apply a second color to the molding, etc., if desired. This can be done best with an artist's brush. Remove as much of the color as you like with clean cloths.

After the second color is dry, the glaze is applied. Brush it on lightly and let it start to stiffen. Then wipe it with a pad of cheesecloth. The usual method is to remove most of the glaze from the center portion, leaving a heavier coating around the edges.

When the glaze is dry, coat with a clear varnish or white shellac.

Blond finishes A blond finish might be defined as a clear or semi-clear finish that is lighter than the natural color of the material to which it is applied. There are numerous finishes of this type: driftwood, honey-maple, and silver-oak finishes are examples. They are mainly used on furniture, woodwork, and wood paneling.

Driftwood finish This is a light-gray, streaked finish used on paneling, woodwork, and furniture. First apply walnut or mahogany oil-stain. The choice depends on whether you want the deep dark undertone made by walnut or the lighter tone of mahogany. Remove the excess after a few minutes. When dry, brush on a coat of white enamel undercoater; work it into the pores; let it stand for a few minutes; then wipe it off. When dry, this should give the desired driftwood color. If not, apply undercoater a second time. Finish with white shellac and/or clear varnish.

French polish A clear finish sometimes used on pianos and other fine furniture. It is made with white shellac diluted to a 1-pound cut (*see* shellac).

The wood must be satin-smooth and absolutely free of dust to start. Roll a soft, lint-free cloth into a small ball; dip it in the thinner shellac and apply to the wood in straight strokes. Allow it to dry for an hour or more, then rub with 4/o steel wool. Apply several more coats in the same way.

When a faint sheen develops in the finish, add four or five drops of boiled linseed oil or pure olive oil to a small quantity of the shellac and apply to the wood with a rotary motion. When dry, sprinkle a little pumice on the surface and rub with a soft cloth dipped in oil.

Continue in this manner, adding a little more oil to each coat of shellac, until you have applied a total of eight or more coats. The final finish should have a deep glow.

Glazes Glazes are transparent coatings applied over previously painted surfaces for decorative purposes. They are usually included in the kits designed for producing antique finishes, but you can make your own glaze by mixing 1 part linseed oil with 3 parts turpentine and whatever pigment you like, such as raw umber, sienna, and black.

Since glaze dries quite rapidly, apply it to only a small section at a time. Put it on with a pad of soft cloth or a brush, and wipe it off with a dry cloth. The depth of the glaze depends on how much you remove. You can get various effects by using a circular, or straight, wiping motion; brushing lightly with a dry brush; or rubbing small spots with a cloth wrapped around a finger.

Heather mahogany finish You can make this furniture finish by bleaching the mahogany and then applying a white paste-filler or white enamel undercoater. Work this into the pores; allow it to stand a few minutes; then wipe it off. When dry, steel-wool lightly and apply shellac and/or varnish.

Honey-maple finish A pleasant light finish for maple or birch paneling, woodwork, and furniture. Mix 1 part white lacquer with 4 parts water-white (clear) lacquer and thin the mixture with equal parts of lacquer thinner. Apply evenly to the wood with brush or sprayer. When dry, finish with two coats of water-white lacquer.

Knotty-pine finish This finish is used mainly on wood-paneled walls, woodwork, and furniture. Ordinarily the wood contains knots, and you just apply a medium-brown stain that is overcoated with shellac or varnish. But it is also possible to fake a pretty good knotty-pine finish on wood that is free of knots.

Mix burnt umber colors-in-oil with a little linseed oil, and paint the knots on the wood with an artist's brush. Use a real knotty-pine board as your guide. Place the knots as much as possible to fit in with the grain of the wood being finished. Outline them first with a pencil.

When the paint has dried, apply an oil stain to the entire surface. Finish with a couple of coats of white shellac; or one coat of shellac and a covering coat of clear varnish.

Limed-oak finish A finish for woodwork, paneling, and furniture. Bleach the oak; sand when dry; and apply a sealer coat of well-thinned white shellac. Fill the pores of the wood with white paste wood-filler or white enamel undercoater. For a protective finish, use white shellac or water-white lacquer.

Linseed-oil finish This is sometimes used on furniture and wood paneling. It is not highly resistant to water but will withstand hot dishes. It is also less likely to show scratches than varnish or other hard finishes. It takes time to apply but gives wood a beautiful, mellow luster.

The application procedure is described under furniture, wood. All rags used in this process should be burned or stored under water. If they are just set aside, spontaneous combustion may occur.

A second kind of linseed-oil finish that is generally not called a finish is frequently applied to wood siding and trim. The purpose is to protect the wood to a certain extent and prevent it from weathering naturally. Application consists simply of brushing a coat of linseed oil on to the wood; letting it penetrate and dry for a week or two; and then brushing on a second coat.

Exterior oil-finishes were more popular in the past than they are today. They have lost ground because in time they usually turn the wood a very dark color; they soil badly; and perhaps worst of all, they mildew badly.

Marble finish This is usually a three-color paint finish applied to furniture. Apply any colors you like. Use an actual piece of marble or a color photograph as your guide; and practice your technique before you get down to brass tacks.

The first step is to apply a solid base-color and let it dry. Then apply a second color with a small soft artist's brush and immediately add the third color with a stiffer paint brush drawn sideways. Blend the colors as desired with another brush, which should be kept dry.

An alternate way to apply the second and third colors is to work with a worn feather. Apply the second color by dipping the feather tip in the paint and drawing squiggly lines on the base color. Blur the paint occasionally. You can then let this dry and apply the third color in the same way; or you can apply the third color while the second is still wet to achieve a really blurred effect.

Pickled-pine finish This finish is not the same to all people. The range of colors usually lies between olive green, gray, and driftwood gray. Some paint manufacturers offer special pickled pine finishes. If you don't use these, one method of making your own finish is to bleach the wood. Then apply a white paste-filler or white enamel-undercoater tinted with raw umber and a little black. Wipe into the pores of the wood and remove the excess. Sand lightly. Finish with two coats of thinned white shellac.

Pickled-pine finish is used mainly on wood paneling and woodwork.

Silver-oak finish A blond finish for oak furniture. Mix 1 part light-gray lacquer with 3 parts clear lacquer, and apply a thin, even coat to the wood. When dry, work a white paste wood-filler into the pores of the wood and wipe off the excess. Sand and then finish with a couple of coats of water-white lacquer.

Spatter finish Spatter finishes are used mainly on floors and flat furniture surfaces. You can spatter paint on paint or paint on any other type of surface. If you have a spray gun, adjust the nozzle so that it gives a very fine spatter effect. A larger, coarser effect is achieved by hand.

Just dip the tip of a brush in paint and, using an overhand stroke, hit the ferrule sharply against a stick held in your other hand. The size of the dots falling from the brush depends on how close the brush is to the painted surface and on how much paint is on the brush. Make a test on newspaper before you begin.

Although it is not essential to protect the finish when dry, it is a good idea. Apply white shellac or a clear varnish.

Stippled finish This is a special wall finish with a dotted effect. It is made with alkyd paints but never with latex, which dries too fast.

Paint the wall the desired background color, using a brush or roller. Let this dry. The color to be stippled is brushed heavily on a sheet of metal or plywood. Then press a slightly damp sponge against the brushed-out paint and press against the wall, thus transferring the paint to the basecoat in an irregular pattern. Repeat this process until the entire wall is covered.

Another way to stipple is to use special stippling brushes or rollers. For a two-tone effect, brush on the basecoat. Then, after this has dried, brush or roll on a contrasting color; and while it is still wet, go over it with the stippling brush or roller. This leaves small areas where the basecolor shows through.

A stippled effect can also be obtained with a single color. This is made by brushing or rolling on the paint and then going over it with a stippling brush or roller while it is wet.

Wax finish A very simple finish for furniture and wood paneling, it can be applied in two ways:

1. Just rub a solvent-based paste wax directly on the wood. This gives some protection but leaves little visible surface film. Unfortunately, if you should ever want to apply another finish, you would have difficulty removing the wax.

2. Seal the wood with a coat of thinned white shellac. Sand when dry and rub on wax.

Wrinkled finish This is a novelty finish designed to give the effect of paint that has wrinkled from age, heat, or improper application. It is often used to decorate metal accessories. It is available in aerosol containers.

how to paint boats

Use top-quality marine paints and finishes for this work. Paints designed for other purposes are not generally suitable for marine work and will not perform satisfactorily. Apply finishes in strict accordance with directions on label.

When you paint a boat, the best rule is to work from the top down. If the mast is stepped, do the top of it first; then the spars; then the rest of the mast; then the cabin top, cabin sides, and deck. Then do the rest of the bright-work and proceed to the topsides and, finally, the bottom. The cabin interior can be finished at anytime. If the mast is not stepped, it can also be done at anytime.

A slightly different procedure followed by some boat owners is to finish the mast, spars, topsides, and bottom (in that order), while the boat is in the yard. Then, after the boat is in water, the rest of the work is completed. The advantage of this procedure is that the fussier finishing work is not exposed to the dusty conditions of a crowded yard.

Basic rules for painting a boat are as follows.

1. Do not apply a finish if the temperature is under 45 to 50 degrees. Some finishes, notably spar varnish, should be applied at even higher temperatures. No finish should be applied if the temperature is over 85 degrees.

2. Make sure all surfaces are completely dry. Wood and plywood require a considerable period of dry weather before the moisture in them evaporates. Do all painting and finishing on dry days only.

3. Apply putty, seam fillers, and glazing compounds after priming bare wood.

4. Never use steel wool on a boat, since the fragments left embedded in the surface will soon rust. Use bronze wool instead.

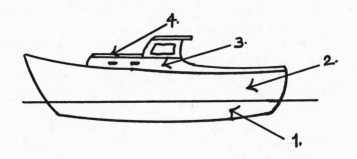

Basic elements of a boat: 1. Bottom. 2. Topside. 3. Super-structure. 4. Deck.

5. Because of the fire hazard, never use a flame or an inflammable paint remover on a boat. To remove old paint, use a sander, scraper, infra-red lamp, or non-inflammable paint and varnish remover.

6. Always clean surfaces with detergent solution, turpentine, etc. before sanding. The heat created by sanding often drives salts and other pollutants into the pores of the material where they may interfere with the adhesion of the later-applied paint.

After sanding, dust and other loose particles can be picked up with a tack rag or vacuum cleaner.

7. Do not use shellac as a primer on boats.

Boot-tops   Paint boot-tops, or waterline stripes, after finishing the bottom and topsides. The lower edge of the stripe is supposed to mark the waterline of the boat when empty, while the top edge marks the waterline when the boat is loaded. To help you paint a straight stripe, apply masking tape to the hull.

Use the same paint for the stripe as used on the bottom, but a different color.

Bottoms   Whether you use an anti-fouling paint or a topside paint on the bottom of your boat depends on the water and climate in which you do your boating; on what sort of boating you do; and on how often you trailer or beach the boat.

Fouling of boat bottoms is mainly a problem in fairly quiet salt water and to a lesser extent in fairly quiet fresh water. But fouling does not occur in fast water or on moving boats.

It follows that anti-fouling paint should be applied to the bottom of your boat if you keep it either in fresh or salt water more or less constantly. But if your boat is normally moored in a strong current or if you pull it out of the water after each use, ordinary marine paints will be satisfactory.

Anti-fouling paints contain a toxicant that kills or discourages any plant or animal growth that tries to attach itself to a boat bottom. In most paints the toxicant, which dissolves very slowly over a period of months, is a copper compound. But inasmuch as copper can cause any bare iron or steel surfaces under a coat to corrode rapidly, knowledgeable boat-owners today use a paint containing a tin compound.

One other important difference between anti-fouling paints is their relative hardness. Conventional formulations are fairly soft and are best used on slow-moving boats and others that are kept moored for considerable periods of time. So-called racing paints are harder and smoother (like the gloss enamel used on bathroom walls). They are recommended for all boats, racing or otherwise, that are operated at high speed because they reduce friction and may actually increase a boat's speed.

The best of the racing bottom paints are made with vinyl.

ALUMINUM BOTTOMS   If an anti-fouling paint is required, use one containing a tin non-galvanic toxicant rather than copper.

Aluminum to be painted for the first time should be washed with a strong detergent solution or household cleanser. Rinse well. Then, because the metal is smooth and non-porous, coat it with a metal etching primer, which not only etches the metal but also serves as a base for the finish coats. The alternative is to apply a phosphoric-acid wash, followed by a water rinse, followed by application of a zinc-chromate metal primer. The bottom is then ready for the final finish.

Aluminum which has been painted before should be cleaned and sanded like a wood bottom (see wood bottoms). Prime bare metal with zinc chromate. Then apply paint.

FIBERGLASS BOTTOMS   If an anti-fouling paint is needed, use a vinyl bottom-paint containing either copper or tin toxicants, depending on whether there is exposed metal under the boat. If underwater growths are not a problem, use the same epoxy paint you would use on topsides or an epoxy primer followed by an alkyd marine enamel

Whatever the finish, it should not be applied to a new fiberglass hull or a hull that has been patched until the fiberglass has cured for at least a week. Then clean the bottom with a strong detergent solution or solvent wash to remove wax, grease, and dirt, which would interfere with paint adhesion. Sand thoroughly with coarse sandpaper, using a rotary motion, to roughen the surface.

Apply vinyl anti-fouling paint directly to fiberglass. Use an epoxy primer under other paints.

On a previously finished fiberglass bottom, simply clean and sand the old finish before applying new. If the finish over a sizable area needs to be taken off, use ordinary paint remover. However, since the remover will attack the fiberglass if left in contact with it very long, work on small sections, take up the remover and softened paint immediately, and neutralize the surface by washing with water.

WOOD BOTTOMS To prepare a wood or plywood bottom for painting, remove growths with a wire brush and wash well. After the surface is dry, go over the bottom with sandpaper or a vibrating sander to remove loose and defective paint. If the paint is in very bad shape, you may have to remove it all with paint remover. Complete removal is also necessary if you intend to apply vinyl bottom-paint because vinyl, like lacquer, attacks other finishes to which it is applied.

Open seams should be filled with caulking material that is recommended for the bottom paint you intend to use. In case no recommendation is made, use vinyl caulking under vinyl paint and urethane or other seam filler for other types of paint.

When all preparation is complete, apply an undercoat to bare wood of the type called for by the paint manufacturer. Then apply one or two coats of finish paint.

Some plywood hulls on small boats are covered with a plastic laminate that often does not hold paint satisfactorily. To correct this problem, the bare plastic must be sanded well but not deeply before paint is applied.

Topsides Instructions for painting topsides are as follows:

ALUMINUM TOPSIDES, DECKS AND SUPERSTRUCTURES Wash new aluminum with detergent solution, then apply a metal etching-primer that both etches and primes the metal. Follow with two coats of epoxy, silicone, or alkyd marine-enamel. Add an abrasive to the final coat applied to decks.

If aluminum has been previously finished, surface preparation can be limited to thorough washing and sanding if the finish is sound. If the finish must be removed down to the metal, a priming coat of zinc chromate should be applied followed by the top coating.

ALUMINUM MASTS AND SPARS For a clear finish, clean the aluminum with a strong detergent solution and, if necessary, a metal conditioner. Use a metal deoxidizer to remove products of corrosion. Then brush on a clear, non-yellowing acrylic lacquer.

If the metal is to be painted, clean as above and etch with a metal conditioner. Then apply an epoxy metal-primer and one or two coats of epoxy enamel.

FIBERGLASS TOPSIDES, DECKS, AND SUPERSTRUCTURES Allow new or patched fiberglass to cure for at least a week. Then clean with solvent solution or strong detergent-solution and sand with coarse sandpaper. These preliminary steps are necessary to assure good paint adhesion. Conceal imperfections in fiberglass with an epoxy primer and glazing compound.

Of the several types of paint that can be applied to fiberglass above the water line, epoxies and silicones are most highly recommended. The former stick tight to fiberglass and have high resistance to abrasion. They must, however, be buffed occasionally to keep them looking their best. The silicones are easy to apply and hold their color and glossy finish extremely well. Both types of paint can be applied directly to fiberglass.

To make decks skidproof, mix an abrasive recommended by the paint manufacturer into the final coat.

To refinish a previously painted surface, follow the same methods as given for finishing bottoms.

STEEL TOPSIDES, DECKS, AND SUPERSTRUCTURES Wash new steel with turpentine or benzine and remove rust and scale, preferably by sandblasting or with a wire brush. Apply two coats of red lead primer; then two or, better still, three coats of epoxy, silicone, or alkyd marine-enamel. Mix an abrasive into the final coat that is applied to a deck.

If painting over an old finish, inspect the surface with care. Take off any loose, peeling, or broken paint with paint remover and a scraper. On exposed metal, remove rust by scraping, filing, and sanding; then use a liquid or jellied rust remover.

Because steel surfaces should be covered with four or more layers of finish, hard sanding is needed around spots of chipped paint in order to remove the sharp, jagged paint edges that would show through a new finish.

Brush two coats of red-lead primer on all cleaned metal before applying the final finish.

WOOD AND PLYWOOD TOPSIDES, DECKS, AND SUPERSTRUCTURES Sand bare wood until it feels velvety smooth. Apply an undercoat that is compatible with your finish enamel to the wood, and sand again when it is dry. On plywood, use a clear or pigmented phenolic-resin sealer to conceal the grain. Apply seam filler or glazing compound after the surface is primed. Finish with two coats of silicone or alkyd enamel. Mixing an abrasive with the final coat of deck paint makes for safer footing.

Wood and plywood can also be finished with epoxy enamel, in which case you should start with an epoxy primer.

Preparation of old painted or varnished surfaces, if sound, consists of washing with strong detergent solution, rinsing, and sanding. A bad finish should be removed completely. Then follow the directions for painting new wood.

Decks Painting of decks is divided into the following categories:

WOOD BRIGHT-WORK AND VARNISHED DECKS Remove the old varnish if it is not in first-class condition. The varnish should also be removed if there are dark spots in the wood. The spots can then be bleached with a solution of ½ cup oxalic-acid crystals in 1 quart hot water. Work in the sunlight if possible and keep swabbing the bleach on the wood until the spots disappear. Then stop the bleaching action and neutralize the area by applying a solution of 1 cup borax in 1 quart of water. Let the wood dry at least 24 hours before sanding.

Open-grained woods, such as oak and mahogany, will look somewhat better and will be easier to seal completely if you apply a paste wood-filler of the desired color. First clean and dust the wood well; then brush the filler across the grain and with the grain. It should be thinned only enough to make it brushable. When it begins to look dull (in about 10 minutes), rub it off across the grain with coarse rags, and keep rubbing until the wood is smooth and even in appearance. Then allow the filler to dry for about 12 hours, and sand lightly.

Use a marine spar varnish to finish the bright-work. A formulation containing urethane is the toughest type but tends to yellow when exposed to the sun.

To seal the wood, the first coat of varnish should be thinned with ⅛ to ¼ part of mineral spirits. On plywood, however, a clear phenolic-resin primer is recommended. The priming coat should be followed with three coats of varnish as it comes from the can. Allow each coat to dry 24 hours before applying the next, and sand and clean the wood thoroughly each time.

New wood that has never been finished is handled in the same way.

If old varnish on wood is sound, there is no need to remove it. You should, however, go over it thoroughly with sandpaper and/ or bronze wool to smooth out laps and roughen the surface. Then apply two coats of marine varnish from the can. One is not enough, no matter how good the old finish.

Varnish that has been carefully applied should last a full season under the worst conditions. It you are a saltwater sailor, however, you will help matters considerably if you sponge off the bright-work after it has been doused with salt water. Each grain of salt left on a clear finish attracts moisture, which acts as a magnifying glass and intensifies the ultraviolet attack on the finish.

CANVAS DECKS AND CABIN TOPS   New canvas is laid in a thick layer of white lead, smoothed out carefully, and allowed to dry. Cover with three coats of alkyd or silicone deck paint. The first and second coats should be thinned according to the manufacturer's directions. Add a skid-proofing abrasive, if desired, to the last coat.

If a canvas deck is worn but in otherwise sound shape, sand it well to remove about as much paint as you intend to apply. Wash the surface with detergent solution and rinse. Then brush on one or two coats of paint

Generally, if the finish on canvas is badly cracked or worn it is better to replace the canvas than to bother refinishing it. You can, however, save it if you remove the old finish down to the fabric. Use paint remover and give it plenty of time to work. Covering it with newspapers for about 30 minutes will retard evaporation of the solvent. Then scrape off the paint very carefully with a dull scraper or putty knife with rounded corners. Wash the cleaned surface with turpentine to neutralize the remover. Brush with a soft wire-brush or stiff bristle-brush to get rid of all crumbs. Then paint like new canvas.

CABIN INTERIORS These can be finished like your boat's topside. Before painting, wash all mildewed surfaces with a strong detergent solution and rinse well. Add a mildewcide to the paint.

Centerboard trunks Use the same paint as that on the bottom. To clean the trunk before painting, attach a long handle to a wire brush and scrub this up and down over all surfaces. If the trunk is too narrow to receive the brush, cut a long, 3-inch-wide strip of ¼-inch wire mesh and, with the aid of an assistant, draw this back and forth inside the trunk. Finish the job with an old wood rasp wired to a lath or with coarse sandpaper tacked to a lath.

Apply paint with a shoe-polish brush, an old paint brush, or a piece of thick-pile carpet attached to a lath.

Motors Clean thoroughly to remove dirt, grease, loose paint, etc. Scrape and sand off rust and clean the metal further with a liquid or jellied rust remover. Prime bare iron or steel with red-lead primer and aluminum with zinc chromate. Finish with one or two coats of engine enamel.

In waters in which fouling is especially severe, lower parts of motors may be treated with anti-fouling bottom paint containing a tin toxicant.

Canoes Most canoes made today are of aluminum or fiberglass and do not require painting. If you want to change the color, however, follow directions for painting boats (aluminum bottoms) and boats (fiberglass bottoms). An anti-fouling paint is not required, since canoes are taken out of the water at the end of the day.

Wood canoes covered with canvas require a finish inside and out to keep them in condition. Use an alkyd marine-paint on the bottom in the way described under boats (canvas decks and cabin tops). If you apply one or two coats of top-quality spar varnish to the wood inside the canoe every year, it should continue in excellent condition for a long time.

If the old varnish finish has been allowed to deteriorate to the point that bare wood is exposed, some stains may have developed. These must be bleached if you want to continue with a clear finish. Then the old varnish should be removed entirely or sanded well to obliterate scars (both jobs are miserable). On the other hand, if you decide to paint the wood simply remove the unsound varnish and wash the entire canoe well. Then brush or spray on two coats of alkyd marine enamel.

how to paint
swimming pools

There are several excellent types of swimming-pool paints available, and only these paints, which are specifically designed and recommended for use on pools, should be used.

One of the most popular and widely used paints for concrete swimming pools are the solvent-thinned or chlorinated rubber-base paints. These will not be harmed by the alkali in concrete or concrete plaster and are easy to work with. Some of the solvent-thinned paints contain vinyl resins and these are difficult to handle and should be applied by a professional.

Catalytic coatings—the two-component epoxy or polyester type swimming pool paints—are excellent for several types of pools but are more difficult to apply than the solvent-thinned rubber-base paints. These produce a coating that is highly durable with excellent resistance to chemicals and alkali.

For metal pools, paints with a phenolic or vinyl system are the best, but these require professional application.

Determining how much paint is needed for a pool is not difficult. It is done by multiplying the length by the height to get the area of a side; width and height to get the area of an end, and width and length to get the area of the bottom. If the bottom slopes, in order to determine the area of side, measure the height at the deep and shallow ends, add together and divide by two; then multiply by the length. Add all the areas together to get the total in square feet.

APPLICATION Paints can be applied to a pool with a brush, roller, or spray gun. Manufacturers of pool paint will specify on the label the recommended method of application and it is wise to follow this suggestion.

No paint should be applied to a pool until the surface is thoroughly dry. If a concrete pool has been full of water for a long period, let it dry for two weeks. Do not paint early in the morning when the surface may still be damp from dew or when rain is expected in the near future. Do not paint when the temperature is below 40 degrees or in the hot sun because it causes lap marks and blistering of the finish. Experienced painters follow the sun, so they keep in the shade. Avoid painting when there is a strong breeze blowing because it will deposit dirt and debris on the fresh paint. Give the paint a week or more to dry before filling the pool.

Concrete and cement plaster pools   The best choice for the amateur is either the solvent-thinned rubber-base paint or an epoxy pool-paint.

New concrete and cement plaster must be allowed to cure for at least two weeks. Then etch all surfaces with a strong solution—around 20 percent—of muriatic acid applied with a stiff scrubbing brush on a long handle. The acid should be kept in contact with the masonry until the foaming of the solution stops. Hose down with lots of water applied in a strong stream.

On old pools if the paint is badly chipped, cracked, or loose, it should be removed, and the only practical way to do this is by sandblasting. After this, scrub the concrete with muriatic acid. If the paint is bad only in spots, however, scrape it off with a stiff putty knife; then go over it with an electric sander and a very coarse grade paper. Scrub off grease, dirt, mildew, and algae with a strong detergent solution, and rinse well. Then scrub with muriatic acid and rinse again.

If the old paint is sound but faded, just wash with detergent solution followed by a mild—5 percent—muriatic acid wash and then rinse again.

Fill all cracks in the pool with a caulking compound. Use a type of compound recommended for use with the particular type of paint you are using. Cracks must be cleaned thoroughly before sealing to insure good adhesion.

Aluminum pools   Clean new metal with a strong detergent solution. Etch it with phosphoric acid and rinse thoroughly. Apply an epoxy pool-primer followed by an epoxy finish coating.

In repainting, etch any metal that is exposed, clean well, roughen the old paint slightly (if it is very slick and smooth), and apply a new coat of epoxy if this was the original finish.

Fiberglass pools   Although these are usually not painted, they may be. Scrub all surfaces with a strong detergent-solution and rinse. Sand vigorously to roughen the fiberglass. Then apply an epoxy pool-primer followed by epoxy finish coating.

Steel pools   If the surface of a new pool is primed, follow the maker's directions for applying the final coats of paint. Thereafter, if the paint film is sound, all you have to do is scrub it clean and apply the same type of paint.

If a new steel pool is not primed, all surfaces must be primed at once. Any rust or corrosion that is present must be removed before painting. This can be done with chemical rust remover or, if the condition is widespread, by sandblasting. Immediately after the bare metal is exposed a metal conditioner should be applied, and, after this treatment, the metal should be primed. An epoxy system is excellent on steel pools.

On old pools, be sure to remove loose paint and rust before repainting. Prime bare metal with a rust-inhibiting primer. The only other thing you must do is clean the old paint and roughen it slightly.

COPING   Use the same type of paint you apply inside the pool. An abrasive may be mixed into the final coat to provide a skid-proof surface.

SUBMERGED METAL EQUIPMENT   Wash with a detergent solution. Remove every speck of corrosion. Prime steel with a metal primer and aluminum with zinc chromate. Then apply epoxy pool-paint.

It is advisable to repaint steel equipment every year, even though the old finish appears to be sound.

WOOD DIVING-BOARDS   First wash the board with a strong detergent solution to remove dirt, grease, mildew, etc. Rinse well and allow the wood to dry in the hot sun for a day or more. Then sand well, cut out splinters, and fill holes with plastic wood.

Prime bare wood with an epoxy primer. Then apply a special epoxy diving-board paint with abrasive added. Stir the paint frequently to keep the abrasive in suspension. Pour the paint directly from the can on the board and spread it around, but don't brush it out too much.

Note that modern diving boards are covered with fiberglass that has a skidproof finish. These are not painted unless you wish to change the colors, in which case use the paint recommended for wood boards.

how to paint
special materials

Bamboo This is most often given a clear finish. You can use varnish, shellac, or lacquer. Before application, clean the surface with a thinner, or, if very dirty, with detergent solution.

Paint will stick better if, after washing, the bamboo is roughened slightly with sandpaper or steel wool. Apply an alkyd primer and enamel.

Canvas Light-weight canvas and drill used in awnings, cushions, beach umbrellas, tents, etc. can be painted with special canvas paint if you can see through the weave when you hold the fabric up to the light. If you can't see through, the fabric will probably not absorb the paint.

Wash the canvas in detergent solution if it is dirty; rinse well and allow to dry completely. Two coats are usually needed for uniform coverage.

Heavy canvas laid on decks is painted with alkyd porch and deck enamel, or a marine deck-paint. Three coats are needed on bare canvas.

China Wash well and dry. Apply an epoxy enamel. It is durable and washable. Gold paint is often used to touch up decorations on china, but it is not very washable.

Cork Wash with detergent solution and let dry at least overnight. Stains that have penetrated the surface are hard to obliterate, but you may have luck if you go over them with medium and then fine sandpaper. For a clear finish, apply two coats of varnish, shellac, or lacquer. For a colored finish, use latex or alkyd paint. All applications are best made by spraying.

Enamelware If you expect to continue using a utensil finished with porcelain enamel for cooking, don't paint it: no finish designed for home application can withstand the heat of a range burner or oven. If enamelware is not used for cooking, however, you can repaint it with any solvent-base gloss or semi-gloss interior enamel or enamel made specifically for metal. Roughen the surface with sandpaper or coarse steel wool first.

Chipped spots on enamelware are painted with an epoxy touch-up enamel.

Fabrics Colors in upholstered furniture, draperies, lamp-shades, and rugs can be renewed (but not changed) with special fabric finishes available in spray cans. The finishes will also obscure most stains, faded streaks, and water marks. Select the color closest to the existing color. A darker shade in the same color family does better at concealing stains and other blemishes than a lighter shade. Test these on a small, inconspicuous area before trying to coat an entire piece.

Before painting, fabric should be vacuumed to remove loose dirt and dust. Clean with a special cleaner recommended by the paint manufacturer.

Fiberglass, rigid The rigid material commonly called fiber-glass is actually a polyester fabric that is reinforced with fiber-glass.

If the rigid fiberglass is new or newly patched, allow it to cure for a week or longer; then wash with detergent solution and rinse. To insure good adhesion of paint, sand the surface hard. Then brush on an epoxy primer and follow with an epoxy or alkyd enamel.

If old paint on fiberglass is in poor condition, it can be taken off with any chemical paint remover. But since the remover will attack the fiberglass if left in contact with it very long, work on only a small area at a time and neutralize the surface immediately.

Glass The most durable paint for glass is an epoxy enamel or liquid acrylic plastic sold by hobby-kit manufacturers. By all means use these if you are decorating objects that must be washed fairly frequently. If the glass is not to be washed, however, an alkyd will do perfectly well.

For a frosted finish on glass, use a paint especially made for this effect, or apply equal parts of paste wood-filler and varnish and stipple it with crumpled paper when it has set a few minutes.

Water paints and inks can be applied to glass if the glass is first sprayed with a colorless lacquer of the type used to "fix" pictures so they won't smudge.

Glass to be painted in any way should be washed in a detergent solution, preferably in a dishwasher. Allow to air-dry or dry with a lint-free cloth. Try not to touch the glass with your fingers.

Ivory If you must finish ivory, apply a clear lacquer, white shellac, or any solvent-base enamel. Wash with soap and water first. If the ivory is discolored, you can bleach it somewhat (before applying a clear finish) by setting it in the sun for a week or so.

Laminated plastics Formica and similar plastic laminates are best painted with an epoxy enamel. Ordinary enamels can be used, but because the plastic surface is extremely dense and smooth, adhesion will not be too satisfactory if the paint is subject to moisture or wear.

Before applying epoxy, scrub the laminate with household cleanser and rinse thoroughly. Dry. Then roughen the surface as much as possible with coarse sandpaper.

Leather To change the color of leather, buy one of the small shoe-coloring kits sold in shoe stores. These contain a leather conditioner and a bottle of paint.

First, scrub the leather with the conditioner, which contains perchlorethylene. Use a clean cloth and rub briskly to remove soil as well as any old polish. Light-colored leather should be washed with detergent solution before the conditioner is used.

After conditioning, allow the leather to dry. Then apply the coloring material with the little pad included in the package or with a soft white cloth. Apply evenly and lightly; allow to dry completely (it takes about ten minutes); then apply a second coat. A third coat may be needed for complete coverage or a deep color.

If leather on a table top or other rigid surfaces is to be given a clear finish, clean it first with a spray-on leather conditioner and allow it to dry. You can then apply, preferably by spraying, several thin coats of water-white lacquer, white shellac, or clear varnish.

Marble It is almost wicked to paint marble. If you insist on doing so, wash it with detergent solution and rinse well. If the surface is slick roughen it with sandpaper. For the most durable finish, brush on an epoxy primer and enamel.

Do not apply a clear, hard finish of any kind to marble with the idea that it will protect the surface. It will spoil the appearance of the stone. Use only a special marble sealer. This is a colorless spray-on or brush-on material that penetrates the pores of the marble and protects the stone against stains and dirt. The finish buffs to a high, slip-resistant luster.

Plastics You can paint rigid plastics but it's pretty much a waste of time to paint flexible types. Even though the finish may stick, it will soon crack and peel off under movement.

Apply any type of solvent-based primer and compatible enamel after washing the plastic in detergent solution and roughening the surface with sandpaper or coarse steel wool.

Pottery Finish pottery dinnerware and kitchen utensils like china. Other objects, such as ornaments and vases, should be washed and dried. You can then apply any type of interior paint, although an alkyd gloss or semi-gloss enamel is recommended for easy application and good durability and washability.

Rattan Wash rattan well to get dirt out of the crevices between the strips, and sand lightly to roughen the surface. If the rattan has been outdoors, it is very possible that the nails holding it together have corroded and stained the surrounding wood, thus necessitating application of a bleach.

Depending on where it is used, rattan should be painted with an exterior trim enamel or gloss or semi-gloss interior alkyd. For a natural finish, apply spar varnish.

Terra cotta Scrub with detergent solution. If the terra cotta has a glaze, roughen it as best you can with sandpaper. Then apply an alkyd paint by brushing or spraying. Whether you use an exterior or interior finish depends on where the object is kept.

Vinyl, rigid Vinyl siding, gutters, and shutters come under this heading. They do not require painting because they have no surface finish; the vinyl is a solid color all the way through. You may, however, change the color of vinyl by washing well and roughening the surface with sandpaper. Then apply an alkyd primer and finish coat.

Wicker If a natural color is desired, coat with white shellac or a clear varnish. The best method of application is with a spray can. The wicker can also be be painted with an aerosol enamel. If the wicker is old, wash it thoroughly before applying any finish and allow it to dry in the sun or a very warm room for 24 hours or more.

If heads of brads or nails used in the wicker are rusted, they should be spot-primed with red lead.

how to paint
almost anything

Air-conditioning ducts In a humid location, such as the basement, air-conditioning ducts may sweat in the summer; and then they may begin to rust. The best way to protect them is to cover them with insulation, which completely prevents sweating. You may, however, simply paint them. Follow directions under galvanized steel. This does not stop sweating, of course, but it should stop rusting.

Air conditioners, room Inside the window, use an interior alkyd enamel. Outside, use an exterior trim enamel. The cabinet should be washed clean and sanded to roughen the existing finish and to smooth down chipped areas. Scrape off rust and touch up the bare metal with red-lead primer.

Andirons Ornamental parts of cast-iron or steel andirons can be painted with a heat-resistant metal enamel, either gloss or flat. Black is the obvious choice of color. Remove loose matter from the metal with a wire brush and wipe clean with paint thinner. Paint can be applied with either a brush or spray can.

Brass andirons and brass ornaments on steel andirons should be cleaned with fine steel wool and household ammonia, which is much easier than using a metal polish. Rinse with water and dry well. Then brush or spray with clear lacquer.

Fire dogs are made of cast iron and are generally not painted, but they may be.

Automobiles Scrape and sand off rust down to the bare metal. Fill dents with plastic steel and sand smooth when hard. Brush an automotive primer on all bare spots and scratches. Choose the primer color that will be easiest to conceal with the finish enamel. Then, if you are simply touching up the finish, apply a touch-up or spray enamel, which is available from an automobile dealer or auto-supply store.

If you repaint the entire car, it must be washed with a strong detergent-solution or washing soda to cut through polish that has been applied. For good measure, wash the surface again with benzine. Then sand every square inch to roughen the old enamel. Prime bare metal with a rust-inhibiting primer.

For the finish coat, use a spray gun and apply an enamel that is formulated for metal. Cover windows with paper or cardboard, and stick masking tape around the edges and over the gaskets. Cover all bright-work with masking tape.

To protect and improve the appearance of chrome and aluminum surfaces, apply a clear spray-on chrome cleaner and protector. Deep scratches in chrome must be freed of rust, primed, and covered with a chrome-finish aluminum paint.

Vinyl fabric inside the car can be painted with a special vinyl finish that is sold in spray cans.

Barbecues A few of the higher priced barbecues have a durable, porcelain-enamel finish that stands up well to weather and heat. True, the finish is very likely to develop chips, but these can be touched up with an epoxy enamel so that they are barely visible.

The majority of barbecues sold, however, are made of lightweight steel with a cheap baked-on factory finish that lasts for a very short time. The heat of the fire, sun, and rain rapidly take their toll. You can, however, preserve barbecues of this kind for a fair number of years if you don't treat them too shabbily, and if you maintain the paint finish on the exterior.

Painting the inside of the firebox, or bowl, is a waste of time. In light-steel braziers the best way to protect this metal is to pour in a deep layer of sand, gravel, or vermiculite. Cast-iron needs no protection.

As soon as exterior surfaces begin to show wear, wash the metal well with strong detergent solution. Sand off rust and loose paint. Apply a red-lead primer to bare metal and follow with a couple of coats of gloss enamel made for metal.

The same treatment is recommended for the inner surfaces of roasting hoods and warming ovens, though the paint will not hold up as well here as on the outside.

For how to maintain stainless steel parts, *see* stainless steel.

Basketball backboards If your children aim to become professionals, finish the backboard with an epoxy primer and two coats of epoxy enamel similar to that used on boats or porches. This will give a very tough, weather-resistant, abrasion-resistant finish.

For less serious players, alkyd primer and exterior trim enamel are adequate.

Paint the basketball hoop with a red-lead primer and black metal-enamel.

Bathroom cabinets Although bathroom cabinets are sold with a durable, baked-on finish, the interior painted surfaces, particularly the shelves, are soon scarred and discolored by spilled medicines, etc To repaint, sand the old finish smooth and wash thoroughly with detergent solution. Then apply two coats of alkyd or metal gloss enamel.

Bathtubs The outside surface of an old-fashioned tub on legs can be painted with any good alkyd enamel. If the metal is bare, apply a metal primer first. Because of the rough surface of the metal, a spray gun or aerosol can is easier to use than a brush.

The interior of any tub can be painted with epoxy enamel. Wash the surface with a detergent and then rub it down thoroughly with a paste made of powdered pumice stone and water. Special attention should be given to rust or green stains around the drains and faucets. These must be removed completely. Rinse the tub with water and allow it to dry thoroughly before painting.

If the finish on a tub is chipped, the spots can be patched with an epoxy touch-up enamel.

Bicycles You will save time and do a better job if you take off as many elements that are not to be painted as possible. These include the wheels, seat, chain, handlebars, and any extras, such as a basket. If this is not done, apply masking tape.

Clean all surfaces with benzine or naphtha. Pay particular attention to those areas near moving parts, since they will almost certainly be coated with oil or grease. Rub all surfaces with steel wool to cut the gloss. If there are areas where the old paint has chipped and the metal has begun to rust, clean with steel wool and a jellied or liquid rust remover. Feather the edges of the paint surrounding the area. Then apply a metal primer. When this is dry, give the spot a coat of the same paint that will be used for the entire surface—an exterior metal-enamel or automotive enamel.

The easiest way to paint a bicycle is to suspend it from a ceiling so you can easily reach all surfaces. An alternate method is to build a rough wood frame to hold it secure. A spray gun or aerosol gives quicker results than a brush.

Ceramic objects   Wash well and dry. Any good alkyd or latex interior paint can be used if the objects are not washed frequently. But an epoxy enamel gives a much more durable, washable finish.

Clothes dryers   Some dryers have a porcelain-enamel on top and a less durable baked finish on the sides. Others have a baked finish on all surfaces.

To repaint a porcelain-enamel top, clean thoroughly and roughen the finish with sandpaper. Then apply, preferably by spraying, epoxy enamel.

If your only problem with the porcelain enamel is a few chipped spots, apply epoxy touch-up enamel.

Over a baked finish, use an enamel designed for metal. Spraying gives best results. Wash and sand the old finish first.

Clothes hangers   The best hangers come with an enamel or clear finish. To repaint them, just wipe off dirt, roughen the old finish with sandpaper, and brush on an alkyd gloss enamel.

On inexpensive unfinished hangers use an alkyd primer followed by alkyd enamel.

Curtain rods   Since it is generally desirable to conceal rods as much as possible, use a color that matches the window frame. An alkyd gloss or semi-gloss enamel gives the best finish. Depending on how easily you can get at the back side of the rods, you can take them down for painting or leave them in place. Apply the paint around the rods, and then smooth it off lengthwise.

Dehumidifiers   Because these electrical appliances draw in gallons of moisture, the finish is subject to wear, and rusting is a frequent problem. So inspect them often.

Remove rust as soon as it appears by sanding and with a liquid or jellied rust remover. Then apply a metal primer and an enamel designed for metal.

If the entire dehumidifier needs to be refinished, clean and sand it well before applying primer and enamel.

Dishwashers Wash and sand the old finish. Cover the controls with newspaper and masking tape. Then apply a gloss or semi-gloss enamel made for metal with a sprayer.

If the porcelain-enamel washtub is chipped, apply an epoxy touch-up enamel.

Drapery hardware *See* curtain rods. All pieces of drapery hardware are painted in the same way.

Dried flowers You can preserve these by spraying them with a transparent, colorless spray available in an aerosol can. Follow the manufacturer's directions.

Driveways Concrete driveways can be stained in several ways. Ideally the work should be done when the concrete is fairly new.

Clean the concrete thorough v th trisodium phosphate and rinse well. If the concrete is der e, it should be etched with muriatic acid and rinsed. Apply a stain made especially for concrete. (It is available from a masonry supplies outlet if not from your paint dealer.) Follow the directions on the container. Generally, however, the procedure is as follows:

First, brush the stain into the concrete with a rather stiff paint brush made specifically for use on stucco and masonry. Brush in well until the foaming stops. To avoid obvious overlaps, brush each new load of stain well back into the area previously covered.

When the driveway is completely stained, let it dry thoroughly; then apply a second coat in the same way. One or two additional coats may be applied if you desire a very deep color.

The finish coat is a sealer designed for use with the concrete stain and sold with it. Just brush it on so the pores are filled.

HOW TO PAINT STRIPES ON DRIVEWAYS You may want to do this to control traffic or provide a basketball court for children. Application is the same regardless of the driveway paving.

Clean the surface with trisodium phosphate. Then paint the stripes with a quick-drying, solvent-base traffic marking paint.

Electric plates To keep from getting paint into electric switches and outlets it is best to remove the plates before you paint them. This also prevents painting the plates tight to the wall so you cannot remove them without chipping the paint around them.

Wipe the plates with detergent solution and clear water to remove soil and hand oils. Sand the surface if it is very smooth.

If the wall is painted, use the same paint on the plates; but if the wall is not painted, apply a semi-gloss alkyd enamel to the plates for easy cleaning.

Don't forget to paint the heads of the screws that hold the plates.

Electric-train tables   For durability and cleanability, use a gloss or semi-gloss alkyd interior enamel over an enamel undercoater. A flat enamel is more restful to look at but much harder to wash. Table tennis paints are excellent for train tables.

Fences, chain link and wire   These are commonly made of galvanized steel or aluminum. Clean by brushing with a broom or spraying with a garden hose. Coat with a primer. Use a high zinc content primer for aluminum and one with zinc dust for galvanized steel. For the finish coat, use an exterior enamel.

The easiest way to apply a finish to this kind of fence is with a roller with a 1½-inch nap. The job goes much faster if two people work together. One applies the paint on one side, and the other follows along on the other side with a dry roller, which will remove excess paint and distribute the rest evenly on that side.

Protect shrubs and grass around the fence with drop cloths. If the fence is surrounded by grass, painting it green will make it less conspicuous.

Fences, rustic wood   Most people let rustic wood fences weather naturally, especially if they are bark covered; but you can speed the process, if you wish, by applying a bleaching stain.

Transparent and opaque oil-stains may also be applied to wood without bark if you want a special effect.

Fences, smooth wood   The best paint to use on smooth wood fences is a self-cleaning house paint. Before painting, brush or wash the fence to remove surface dirt. Cut down any vegetation along the base that might interfere with the work.

The easiest way to paint a fence, especially one with pickets, louvers, latticework, and the like, is with a spray gun. Aim the gun at a sharp angle so that most of the paint will strike a solid surface and only a little passes through the openings. Use plenty of drop cloths to protect grass, shrubs, and flowers.

File cabinets   Take off handles and guide rods. Remove

drawers and stand them front up. Clean all surfaces with detergent solution and roughen them slightly with sandpaper. Then apply a solvent-base semi-gloss enamel made for metal or an interior alkyd enamel. Use a sprayer, if possible.

You can either paint around the card holders or paint right over them, which is much easier.

Fire escapes Use an exterior enamel recommended for metal over a suitable metal primer. Remove all loose rust and treat the metal with a metal conditioner before priming. *See* steel. The best way to apply paint to the railings is with a painter's mitt. This permits you to coat the outside surfaces without leaning over the railing or working on a ladder.

Fireplaces The only parts of a conventional built-in fireplace that are normally painted are the breast and mantel. If these are of brick or stone, apply an interior latex or alkyd semi-gloss paint. On wood surfaces use an alkyd semi-gloss. Thorough cleaning to remove dust, soot, etc. is necessary before painting.

Sometimes the inside walls of a fireplace are surfaced with very ugly bricks. These can be made less objectionable if you scrub them hard and then brush on a heat-resistant flat black enamel designed primarily for metal.

Free-standing metal fireplaces are painted at the factory with a heat-resistant finish, usually porcelain enamel. If these ever require refinishing, wash the surfaces well and sand lightly. A heat-resistant enamel designed for metal is the best finish; but you can also use epoxy enamel.

Metal flues of free-standing fireplaces and metal hoods over built-in fireplaces are painted in the same way. *Also see* hearths.

Fireplace tools Fireplace tools and fenders made of steel or cast iron should be cleaned thoroughly and sanded to remove rust. Spot-prime bare metal with a heat-resistant primer. Then apply a solvent-base flat black paint or a heat-resistant metal paint.

Remove tarnish and soil from brass fireplace equipment by scrubbing with fine steel wool and household ammonia. Rinse and dry. For a tarnish-proof finish, spray on a couple of coats of clear lacquer. *Also see* andirons and firescreens.

Firescreens If the screen is made of black iron, brush off the dirt and wash under a hose. Hang in the sun or in front of a fire to dry. Then apply any solvent-base flat black paint; however, a heat-resistant paint designed for metal is best.

Although it is wasteful of paint, spraying will give faster, more uniform coverage than brushing.

Brass firescreens, which are rare, and brass parts on iron screens can be sprayed with a clear lacquer after cleaning with steel wool and household ammonia.

Fishing rods   Modern fishing rods made of fiberglass are not finished. Old steel rods should be rubbed down with steel wool to remove loose finish and rust. Prime with a metal primer; then apply a gloss enamel made for metal.

Bamboo rods with thread bindings are more difficult to finish and require it more often. If the old varnish is imperfect only in spots, scrape it off carefully with a knife; but if the entire finish is bad, the only thing you can do is to apply a water-wash paste remover. Allow this to soften the varnish completely; then wipe it off with a wet rag. Avoid scraping as much as possible, because this can wreck the bindings. Then brush on a couple of coats of spar varnish.

Flowerpots   Use an exterior enamel—latex, oil-base or a masonry paint. Wash the surface thoroughly and allow to dry. As the clay is somewhat porous, several coats will be required to get even coverage. Apply with a brush or spray can.

Flue tile   These are occasionally used to build walls and make planters. Tiles that are glazed are best finished like ceramic tile—with an epoxy enamel. Unglazed tiles can be finished with any good interior or exterior paint, though epoxy will prove to be the most durable. On the other hand, if an unglazed tile is used as a planter, apply an exterior latex paint, which will pass any moisture that escapes through the tile.

For a clear finish on flue tiles used outdoors, apply spar varnish. Indoors you can also use shellac or lacquer.

Franklin stoves   Scrub with detergent solution. Remove rust and prime the bare metal with a heat-resistant metal primer. Then paint the entire stove with a heat-resistant gloss or flat black enamel designed for metal.

Furnaces   Use an alkyd interior gloss paint to refinish the enameled steel cabinet in which a modern furnace, or boiler, is housed. Before applying, you should, of course, clean and sand the old finish; remove rust, and prime the bare metal with a metal primer.

If cast-iron or steel doors on furnaces are to be finished, clean them well and brush on a heat-resistant primer and heat-resistant topcoat made for metal.

Garbage cans   Plastic cans should not be painted because they are too flexible to hold a finish. Aluminum cans are generally not painted either, but may be to improve their appearance. Follow directions under aluminum.

Galvanized-steel cans do not need paint when new, but in the course of time they often lose their zinc coating and begin to rust. The best way to protect the metal inside a can is to brush on a thin coat of non-fibered asphalt roofing cement. Special surface preparation is unnecessary so long as the metal is clean and dry. Take particular care to work the asphalt into the joint between the walls and bottom.

For appearance's sake, you can paint the outside of galvanized garbage cans as directed under galvanized steel.

Kitchen garbage cans are made either of plastic or aluminum and need no refinishing. However, the enamel on garbage can holders often becomes scratched and scarred. In that case, scrub well; remove rust and prime the bare metal; then cover the holder with an alkyd interior gloss-enamel.

Garbage disposals   It doesn't take very long for a disposal, in its vulnerable position under the kitchen sink, to become pretty badly soiled and scarred. Scrub it with strong detergent-solution and rinse. Go over the old baked-enamel finish with sandpaper. Then apply a couple of coats of alkyd gloss-enamel.

Garden tools   Paint is applied to the handles of hand tools so they will be more visible when you lay them down in leaves, tall grass, etc.; and it is applied to the housing, handles, and wheels of power tools to protect them against corrosion.

On wood parts use an alkyd exterior trim paint. Red, orange, and yellow are the best colors because of their high visibility. As long as the wood is clean and dry, no particular preparation is necessary, since the new paint will be worn off rather quickly anyway.

Wash metal surfaces with benzine to remove grease and soil. Remove every speck of rust wtih a scraper, steel wool, and rust remover. Prime bare metal with metal primer. Then apply a farm machinery enamel or a gloss enamel formulated for metal; but on engine surfaces that get extremely hot, use a heat-resistant metal primer and topcoat.

Gunstocks Gunstocks come with a factory-applied finish. When this begins to fail, strip it off with paint remover or by sanding. Then apply spar varnish or a clear finish made especially for gunstocks. One of the best finishes is linseed oil because it is less likely to show scratches than surface coatings, and it can easily be renewed. *See* furniture, wood. The old gunstock formula is to apply linseed oil every day for a week, every week for a month, every month for a year, and every year thereafter.

Hearths Ceramic-tile hearths are not finished in any way. Stone, slate, brick, and unglazed quarry-tile hearths are often left unfinished, too; but they can be made more resistant to soil and stains if you scrub them with a strong detergent solution, rinse, and apply a couple of coats of clear masonry-sealer. On a marble hearth, use a sealer especially formulated for marble.

If you want to change the color of a hearth, apply epoxy floor enamel. *Also see* fireplaces.

Heating ducts Ducts are usually painted only for esthetic reasons, when you use your basement as a family room, and so forth. Follow directions under galvanized steel, and aluminum.

Kitchen cabinets Whether the cabinets have a clear or opaque finish, the first step in the tedious and rather difficult job of refinishing them is to remove the shelves (if possible), hardware and drawers, and wash all surfaces carefully with a strong detergent solution or washing soda. Rinse well.

Sand the cabinets to smooth out scratched and chipped areas and to scarify all other areas so the new finish will hold tight. Spot-prime bare steel with a rust-inhibiting primer.

For a paint finish, use a semi-gloss alkyd interior enamel. The best clear finish is a colorless lacquer; but inasmuch as lacquer sometimes attacks varnish, test it on a small area to make sure the old finish will hold up under it. If it doesn't, you should either refinish the cabinets with spar varnish or cover the old finish with a sealer coat of shellac followed by lacquer.

To achieve the smoothest possible surface, the new finish should be applied with a spray gun. This means that all surfaces in the vicinity of the cabinets must be tightly covered. Use rolls of kraft wrapping paper, if possible; otherwise, use newspapers. Fasten masking tape around the edges of the cabinets. Cover the floor with drop cloths.

Kites   On the wood frame, apply two thin coats of spar varnish; or if you want vivid color, seal the wood with shellac and apply a pigmented lacquer.

Designs are best applied to paper sails with water colors or poster paint. On fabric, use the same paint or a special fabric finish.

Lamps   For the type of paint to use, *see* the entry for the material of which the lamp is made. Generally it is best to use a gloss or semi-gloss, solvent-base enamel (alkyd is excellent) for an opaque finish; use lacquer for a clear finish.

Clean the lamp to remove soil and hand oils. If the lamp is fairly easy to take apart, it is a good idea at least to remove the socket and harp from the base before painting the latter. And even though any lamp is easier to paint when it is standing upright, it is also a good idea to take a lamp completely apart if it is made of several materials and is of intricate design.

Lampshades   Paper, parchment, and plastic lampshades can be painted with a flat or gloss solvent-base enamel. Spraying is the best method of application. Paint the inside as well as the outside so that stains will not show through.

Fabric shades are painted with a special fabric spray (*see* fabrics, special materials).

Laundry tubs   Only an epoxy paint will hold on the interior of the tub. Wash the surface with detergent solution and then scrub it with water and powdered pumice to insure removal of all grease and soap film. Let dry for 24 hours. Then apply two coats of epoxy.

The same paint is best for the exterior of a tub, but it is not absolutely required. An alkyd enamel will do well on a cast-iron tub; use latex on a stone tub.

Lavatories   *See* bathtubs. Porcelain surfaces on lavatories are painted in the same way—with epoxy paint.

Lavatory cabinets are refinished with alkyd gloss or semi-gloss enamel. Lacquer or varnish is used for a clear finish. Be sure the old finish is completely free of soap film, grease, stains, etc.

Lawns   When grass turns brown in the fall, it can be turned green once more with a special color concentrate that is mixe with water. Application is made on a dry day with any garden sprayer or paint sprayer. Use enough spray to cover each blade completely. The tint should last until the following spring, but can be renewed at any time if it does not. The grass is not harmed.

Many golf courses, race tracks and other public establishments tint their lawns. A growing number of home owners, especially those with zoysia grass, are beginning to follow suit.

Color concentrates for lawns are sometimes called "lawn tints" or "lawn dyes." They are sold through garden supply stores as well as paint shops.

Lighting fixtures Disconnect lighting fixtures and take them down from the wall or ceiling before painting. Wash thoroughly with detergent solution: it's amazing how much dust and grease most fixtures accumulate.

Use the finish recommended for the material of which each fixture is made (*see* brass, aluminum, pewter, etc.). A solvent-based semi-gloss or gloss enamel is generally best if you want an opaque finish. Lacquer is best for a clear finish. Apply by spray if possible, but take care not to get the finish on the contact points in the socket.

Inside surfaces of cornice lights, cove lights, large recessed lights, and luminous ceiling-panels should be painted a flat white to increase lighting efficiency and to insure that the light reflected from the surfaces will be white. (Light reflected from a colored surface will be tinted the same color and will distort the appearance of walls and other room surfaces it strikes.)

Mailboxes If a box is new, let it weather for six months; then coat it with a zinc-dust primer (*see* galvanized steel) and finish with two coats of solvent-base exterior enamel, or a gloss enamel made for metal. Use the same kind of paint, but of a contrasting color, to apply your name or house number. You can also use a fluorescent or phosphorescent paint for high visibility.

If a mailbox is old, remove rust and prime the bare metal with a metal primer before applying the finish coats.

Maps Spray with the same kind of lacquer fixative used on pictures. *See* pictures. If you want to make a map look old, apply varnish.

Metal tile Some tiles have a baked-enamel finish; on others, the metal is exposed. In either case, scrub the tile, which is usually used on bathroom and kitchen walls, with detergent solution. Take extra pains to remove brown water stains and gunk in the grouted joints. Roughen the surface slightly by sanding. Finish with an epoxy primer and epoxy enamel. Other solvent-based paints can also be used, but they will not resist moisture and abrasion as well.

Mirrors If the finish on the mirror is damaged, let a glass dealer resilver it or replace it.

To paint a frame, remove the mirror if this is not too difficult. Otherwise, apply masking tape around the edges of the mirror. Use any finish suitable to wood or metal furniture.

Mobile homes Paint like aluminum siding that has a baked-on factory finish (*see* aluminum, metals).

Models Finishes for airplanes, automobiles, and other scale models and toys are more commonly carried by toy and bicycle shops than by paint stores. There are various finishes that can be used.

Probably the favorite is a lacquer product called dope. Start with a clear primer coat applied directly to the model (a dope primer containing a filler is available for balsa and other porous wood). Build up from there with thin coats of pigmented dope until the desired depth of color and shade have been attained. Sand or steel wool each coat with fine sandpaper or wool, and finish with No. 600 sandpaper.

Another way to finish models is to prime the surface with dope. Then apply several coats of a conventional lacquer or enamel. If you start with lacquer, stick with it; similarly, if you start with enamel, stick with that.

Dope is applied with a brush; other finishes are available for brush or spray can application.

Dope should never be applied over any other type of finish because it will destroy it.

Motorcycles *See* automobiles, for repainting painted surfaces and chrome, for protecting chrome surfaces. Several aerosol sprays are available for changing the color of motorcycle seats and other vinyl surfaces.

Oil tanks Oil tanks, which are usually located in the basement or utility room, do not require painting to protect the metal; but paint does improve their appearance and make them easier to keep clean.

Some tanks have a protective asphalt coating. To test whether this is paintable, wipe a small area with a cloth dampened with a solvent paint thinner. If the cloth picks up a black tar-like substance, the finish contains asphalt and must be sealed with aluminum paint before you apply a finish coat of alkyd or latex paint.

If there is no coating on the metal or if the existing coating does not contain asphalt, treat the tank as you would any steel object. Remove all traces of dirt and rust, wash with a strong detergent solution, rinse, and allow the tank to dry. Then apply metal primer and metal enamel.

Pianos   A fine piano has a factory-applied finish that is virtually impossible to duplicate in the home. If such a piano requires refinishing, have the work done by a professional. But if the piano has no great value, you can try applying a clear finish like those described under furniture, wood. Better still, apply enamel.

Clean the surface with a solvent thinner to remove all traces of grease and dirt. If the veneer has come loose, reglue it. If some of the veneer is missing, fill in with plastic wood or water putty and sand smooth. Areas with checked or cracked veneer should be filled with a paste wood-filler and sanded.

To ensure a good bond between the old finish and new enamel, it is best to apply an enamel undercoater. When this dries, sand it with fine sandpaper and apply the first coat of enamel. Let this dry, sand lightly, and apply a second and possibly a third coat of enamel to produce a hard, durable finish.

Care must be taken to keep the paint off the keys and sound box. This risk can be reduced by applying the enamel with a brush rather than a spray gun.

Picture frames   Remove the picture and glass. Stick several thumbtacks part way into the back of the frame so that when you lay it flat it will be slightly elevated above your work table. Clean the frame with ammonia and water and rinse well. On ornate, molded frames, first blow off the dust with a vacuum cleaner and then use a soft paint brush to work the ammonia into the crevices. Let the frame dry completely.

If the frame has a smooth surface, sand it lightly so the new paint will stick. Then brush or spray on an alkyd enamel, furniture varnish or shellac. Gilt frames are redone or retouched with gilt paint or a gold paste that is applied with your finger tip. Both materials are sold by art supply stores.

Pictures   It is often desirable or necessary to apply an invisible finish to water colors, pastels, charcoal drawings, and other pictures to protect them from smudging, moisture, and soil. If the picture is valuable, let an art supply dealer do the work. But you can take care of less important pictures yourself with a nonglossy, spray-on fixative available from art stores. Hang the picture on a wall or other vertical surface that is protected with newspapers; hold the spray can a foot away; and apply the spray with a side-to-side motion. Make several light applications rather than one thick one.

Ping-pong tables   Use a chalkboard or table-tennis paint to renew an old table or paint a new one. These finishes are available in an aerosol spray as well as for application by brush or roller.

Pipes and valves   If you paint pipes and valves to conceal them, apply the color of the ceiling or wall behind them. If you paint them to call attention to them so you won't hit your head when you walk through the basement, use yellow. If you paint them to identify them, use red on heating pipes; orange on hot water pipes; green or blue on cold water pipes. Paint valves yellow if they are hard to find.

Dust and wash the pipes and valves before painting. Remove rust. Apply a red-lead primer to black iron and a zinc-dust primer to galvanized steel. Copper and brass do not need priming.

The finish coat on plumbing pipes and valves should be a gloss enamel made for metal. On heating pipes, especially steam pipes, it is advisable to use a heat-resistant metal enamel.

One point to consider before painting pipes is that those carrying cold water often sweat in summer, especially where they run through damp areas. Paint applied to them will peel off rather rapidly.

Planters   Although planters are made of many materials with varying degrees of resistance to the passage of moisture, it is generally wise in all cases to coat the exterior with latex paint, which will not blister if any water seeps through the planter walls behind it.

Do not treat wood planters with a preservative to make them rot-resistant: the chemical may injure or kill the plants.

Radiators   Radiators should never be given a coat of aluminum or bronze paint, because this reduces the heat output. However, if a radiator already has such a finish, it is not necessary to remove it to increase heating efficiency: just overcoat the metallic finish with a wall paint.

Paint radiators the same color as the adjacent wall to make them less conspicuous. Use any ordinary alkyd interior finish but preferably a semi-gloss, which is readily washed. Latex can be used only on a radiator that has previously been painted with a solvent-based finish. Latex applied directly over bare metal will cause rusting.

The easiest method of applying paint is with a spray can or spray gun. Use large sheets of cardboard to protect the wall and floor. If you use a brush, select one with long bristles about 1½ inches wide, and with a long handle. Paint the hard-to-reach interior surfaces first.

You will find it easier to paint a radiator if it can be disconnected and pulled out from the wall. To disconnect a steam radiator, close the shut-off valve and loosen the large nut with a pipe wrench. Hot-water radiators must be drained before they are disconnected.

Allow a radiator to cool before you paint it. Clean it thoroughly. Use a long-handled brush or the wand attachment of your vacuum cleaner. Wash dirty surfaces.

If the radiator has been previously painted and the paint is sound, fresh paint can be applied directly to it. But if the old paint is cracked and peeling, remove it entirely.

Sand rusted metal and coat it with a metal primer. If the metal has not rusted, you can cover it directly with an ordinary primer.

A new radiator must be cleaned thoroughly to get rid of grease, oil, and pipe dope. Use a solvent paint thinner.

Ranges   Because they must be resistant to heat and acids, modern ranges have a very durable, slick porcelain-enamel finish. Don't try to apply any new finish over this, because even if you can make it stick, it will not hold up well for very long.

However, small chipped spots in the porcelain should be repaired promptly. Just clean them well and apply a little epoxy touch-up enamel.

Finish old cast-iron stoves as you would Franklin stoves.

Record players and speakers If made of wood, follow directions for finishing furniture, wood. Refinish metal cabinets with enamel made for metal. Wash and sand well first.

Refrigerators Use an enamel designed for metal. The best results are achieved if the enamel is applied by spray can or spray gun, but you can do a perfectly adequate job with a brush.

If the refrigerator is recessed in a wall, pull it out so you can easily get at the sides as well as the front. Wash all surfaces with household detergent solution. Then go over them with medium steel wool to cut the gloss so the new enamel will make a good bond. If there are any areas where the old finish has failed and the metal is exposed, remove all traces of rust, sand down the edges of the surrounding paint to produce a feather edge, and then prime with a metal primer. When this is dry, apply a coat of finish paint to build these areas up to the level of the surrounding surface.

If the interior of a refrigerator is to be painted, turn off the motor and remove the contents. After washing, be sure to allow ample time for all surfaces to dry and reach room temperature before painting. And leave the door open after painting to insure proper drying of the new enamel and to allow the paint odors to dissipate. (Note, however, that many modern refrigerators are lined with solid vinyl rather than steel. This should not require painting.)

One complete coat of enamel usually produces a like-new finish.

Registers Paint registers to match the walls or floor. Use a flat wall paint, wall enamel, or metal enamel. The best method of application is with a spray gun.

Remove the registers before painting. They are usually held in place with two or more machine screws or bolts. Dust well to remove all traces of loose matter. Washing with detergent solution may also be necessary.

Most registers have a factory-applied finish and should be roughened slightly with sandpaper. If the existing finish is sound, apply the new paint right over it. If there are rust spots, clean them off and apply a metal primer.

Rugs You can renew but not change the color of wool,

nylon, or any other fabric in a rug or carpet with a spray-on fabric finish. *See* fabrics. Spots that are worn down to the backing can be colored to match the pile with a fabric dye.

Grass rugs can usually be dyed, too; but for a more intense color, apply a spray-on enamel.

Rush Rush is most commonly used for chair seats, and it usually is not finished because a finish makes it stiff and somewhat brittle. On the other hand, a finish does make the rush easier to clean with a sponge.

To prevent excessive stiffness, apply a thin, clear lacquer of the type used on wallpaper or to fix paintings. Two coats should be enough, but they may have to be renewed about every six months, depending on the amount of wear.

Sandboxes Sandboxes need to be repainted every year if you want them to look half-way decent.

To prevent decay, wood boxes should be made of redwood or pine that has been treated with a paintable wood preservative. In the spring, empty the box or mound the sand in the center, and clean the wood inside and out with a brush. Washing may be called for. Let the wood bake out in the sun for several days; then brush on one or two coats of solvent-based exterior trim enamel.

A steel sandbox must be emptied every spring and cleaned well. Remove rust and prime the bare metal with red lead. Overcoat with a gloss enamel made for metal. A couple of coats are needed for maximum protection.

Screens Paint wood frames on screens every two to four years, or as necessary, with exterior trim paint. Aluminum frames with a baked-on finish should not need to be painted more than once every ten years, if that often. Use a trim paint. Unfinished aluminum frames may not need painting in some areas; but in others, you should apply some sort of finish every few years to keep the metal from forming an unattractive rough oxide. Follow directions under aluminum.

Plastic and fiberglass screen cloth should not be painted. But copper should be refinished every year or two to prevent the metal from turning green and staining the frame and wall surface below. Galvanized-steel screen cloth must be painted on the same schedule to control rusting Aluminum screen cloth, like aluminum frames, may or may not need finishing; but it is generally advisable.

To paint screen cloth of any kind, brush it well on both sides to remove loose dirt; then wash under a hose and allow it to dry thoroughly. Use a prepared screen paint or exterior trim paint if you want to color the screen cloth. For a natural finish, use spar varnish. The paint or varnish is most easily brushed on the cloth with a piece of carpet. Apply it liberally to both sides, but take pains not to close up any of the openings.

Shoes   *See* leather. Suede, patent, fabric, and synthetic shoes are colored like leather shoes.

Shower stalls   The durability of the factory finishes applied to the walls of metal shower stalls varies considerably with the basic quality of the stalls. You should examine the walls frequently to make sure the finish has not cracked, chipped, or worn thin. If there are any breaks, sand the finish down to the metal and apply a red-lead primer. Then overcoat with a gloss metal-enamel, preferably applied by spray can or gun.

For how to paint tile walls, *see* ceramic tile.

Shuffleboard courts   Scrub the concrete hard with trisodium phosphate. If the surface has been given a hard, troweled finish, etch it with muriatic acid. Apply two coats of solvent-thinned rubber-based floor enamel with a roller or brush.

Sinks   Paint as you would bathtubs—with an epoxy enamel. The same finish is used on stainless-steel sinks.

Skis   Most skis made today are plastic and do not require painting. On wooden skis apply urethane varnish to the top and edges after removing the old finish completely.

Sleds   Remove rust from metal parts; spot prime with red-lead primer; and overcoat with a gloss enamel made for metal.

Wood parts should be kept coated with spar varnish. Urethane varnish is even more durable but tends to yellow when exposed to sunlight.

Snowblowers   Snowblowers may need repainting every spring before you put them in storage. Paint as you would the metal surfaces of garden tools (*see* garden tools).

To insure that wet snow will not clog in the chute, take pains to remove all rust and other roughness from inside. Then prime with red lead and overcoat with a high-gloss enamel designed for metal. Brushing melted paraffin over the enamel is advisable.

Snowmobiles Paint the same as snowblowers. *See* chrome for how to protect chrome parts.

Soap dishes Wash to remove the soap film, and scarify the surface as best you can with emery cloth. Then apply epoxy primer and gloss epoxy enamel.

Stove pipes Wash with detergent solution if dirty. Remove rust with steel wool. Roughen the old finish. Brush a heat-resistant red-lead primer on bare metal. Then apply a topcoat of heat-resistant enamel made for metal.

Swings and sliding boards Scrape off rust and clean the metal further with steel wool and liquid or jellied rust remover. Brush red-lead primer on the bare metal. Then repaint the entire structure with a gloss enamel made for metal.

Stainless steel slides should not be painted. Galvanized slides, however, may eventually require regular painting to prevent rusting and keep them smooth. Use two coats of metal paint.

Wood seats can be finished with spar varnish or with the same enamel used on the metal.

Television sets Wood cabinets should be refinished like fine wood furniture. *See* furniture, wood. Metal and plastic cabinets must be washed with detergent solution and sanded to roughen the surface slightly. Apply a solvent-based primer and compatible enamel.

Tents *See* canvas.

Tires Paint tires black with a special thin paint called tire black. A white paint of different formulation, but which sticks equally well to rubber, is used to paint white sidewalls. Both paints are applied to the rubber after it has been washed and dried. Use a brush.

Toilet seats Don't expect any finish you apply to a toilet seat to last. Replacing a discolored or damaged seat with a solid plastic seat is recommended. But if you are in an economical frame of mind, try your luck with an epoxy enamel.

First wash the seat well and roughen the surface with sandpaper. Then apply an epoxy primer and enamel.

Tools, workshop Metal surfaces that are to be painted must be free of rust and coated with red-lead primer. Then apply a gloss enamel made for use on metal.

On wood, use spar varnish or the same gloss enamel that is applied to metal.

Toys Do not use finishes containing lead, antimony, arsenic, cadmium, mercury, selenium, or soluble barium, all of which are likely to be harmful if chewed or swallowed.

Clean toys thoroughly and sand smooth. An interior alkyd gloss-enamel or an enamel made for metal can be used on all surfaces and materials.

Toy soldiers Special very-fast-drying lacquers are made for use on both metal and plastic soldiers. They have a dull finish which resembles clothing better than a gloss. To paint soldiers, apply a special gray primer first. Follow with one or two topcoats.

Trays Wash well and sand smooth. Select the finish that is going to be most durable. These are as follows:

For a wood tray, bar varnish or epoxy enamel. Alkyd enamel will also perform well.

For a steel or aluminum tray, an enamel designed for metal.

For a plastic tray (to change the color), epoxy enamel.

Don't use any finish on silver, pewter, and brass trays, for even though a clear lacquer will prevent tarnishing, it won't last long.

Trees When branches are cut from trees, the wounds should be painted to keep out disease germs. The paint is applied as soon as the sap stops running. Special tree paint, usually in aerosol cans, is available at garden supply stores; but any solvent-base house paint does just as well. You can also use asphalt roofing cement.

To make trees growing near a road or driveway more visible, brush or spray on a ring of white house paint.

Trellises Because garden trellises have a lot of joints in which moisture settles; because they are exposed to constant weathering by the sun, rain and snow; and because the vines growing on them tend to trap moisture, which encourages decay, these simple structures require an inordinate amount of painting. And to make matters worse, the work is not easy.

To begin with, trellises should always be made of wood that is resistant to decay; and they should be put together with galvanized nails and screws, which are slow to rust. Horizontal members should be slightly rounded or sloped on top so water runs off readily.

Take the vine down off the trellis before painting. If you can't do this, prune it in late winter or early spring and paint the trellis before new growth starts. In any case, clean the trellis as much as possible with detergent solution, and then rinse and allow the wood to dry thoroughly. Scrape and sand off flaking paint. Fill cracks in the wood with putty or plastic wood.

If the old paint is badly worn, apply an alkyd primer and fol low with a coat of alkyd trim enamel. Over a sound finish, use enamel only.

If the trellis is stained rather than painted, it will need less frequent attention. But when the time comes to refinish, proceed in the same way. Apply a clear or pigmented oil-stain; not a creosote stain, which will injure plants.

Venetian blinds   Paint these with enamel applied by spray can or spray gun. Take the blinds apart and clean them well with detergent solution. Hang the slats on hook-shaped wires so you can paint all sides and edges in one operation.

Washing machines   On the best automatic washers the tops, lids, and tubs are finished with durable porcelain-enamel; the cabinets are finished with a baked enamel. On less expensive models, baked enamel is used on everything except the tubs.

You can refinish porcelain-enamel (after it has been washed and sanded) with a spray-on epoxy enamel. Use a touch-up epoxy to repair chipped spots.

Areas covered with baked enamel are coated with an enamel designed for metal. For the smoothest finish, use a spray gun or aerosol. The finish must be washed and sanded first.

Wastepaper baskets   *See* the entries for the materials of which the baskets are made.

Water heaters   Wash with detergent solution to remove dirt and grease. Remove rust and prime the bare metal with red-lead primer. Apply an enamel designed for metal with a spray can or gun.

Water pumps   Water pumps, including swimming pool pumps, are often installed in damp locations. Consequently, the paint finish applied at the factory soon deteriorates and rust sets in.

In time, you may decide it's a losing battle trying to keep a pump looking well; but until then, check it frequently. Remove rust as it appears and apply a couple of coats of red lead. Then apply two coats of gloss enamel designed for metal.

Water skis Apply two coats of alkyd or epoxy boat paint or two or three coats of marine spar varnish.

Water tanks For how to paint, *see* galvanized steel. However, painting is inadvisable because tanks filled with cold water will sweat excessively in summer, and no finish can last very long.

Window boxes As long as the wood or metal of which a window box is made is sound, repainting is a simple matter of washing the box well and brushing on a new coat of exterior trim enamel. When wood starts to rot, however, repainting is a waste of time. Either replace the defective wood or the entire box.

Rust spots on metal boxes should be cleaned thoroughly when you find them. Then brush on a red-lead primer and overcoat with exterior trim enamel.

Window shades Cloth shades can be painted with oil or latex paint. A preliminary test is always recommended. For this use a sample scrap of shade cloth. If that is not available, unroll the shade all the way and work on the very top inch or two—the portion that is normally wrapped around the roller.

The shade should be unrolled on a large table or the floor for painting. The best method of application is with an aerosol. Apply two or three thin coats rather than a single thick one.

Woodenware Woodenware used in cooking and serving food is usually left unfinished, at least in those areas that food touches. There is, however, no rule about this. If you want to finish such pieces, just be sure not to use any finish containing lead. Generally a clear or pigmented lacquer will do best.

Woodenware to be finished must, of course, be washed and dried thoroughly. Soak grease spots with a cloth dipped in turpentine; but if a salad bowl has been exposed to a great deal of oil, leave it unfinished.

index

Note: For how to paint specific objects and materials, first look for desired item as main entry in alphabetical order in index. If item is not found, then see main entry "How to Paint," or relevant subentry, such as "boats"; "floors"; "furniture"; "masonry"; "metals"; "wood."

26605

t anything.